Unlocking the Power of Your Purpose

John W. Stanko

Unlocking the Power of Your Purpose
by Dr. John Stanko
Copyright ©2015,2022 Dr. John Stanko

All rights reserved. This book is protected under the copyright laws of the United States of America. This book may not be copied or reprinted for commercial gain or profit. The use of short quotations or occasional page copying for personal or group study is permitted and encouraged. Permission will be granted upon request.

Unless otherwise identified, Scripture taken from the HOLY BIBLE, NEW INTERNATIONAL VERSION®. Copyright © 1973, 1978, 1984 by International Bible Society. Used by permission of Zondervan Publishing House. All rights reserved.

Scripture quotations marked NASB are taken from the Holy Bible, New American Standard Bible, copyright © 1960, 1971, 1977, 1995, 2020 by The Lockman Foundation. All rights reserved.

ISBN 978-1-63360-255-7
For Worldwide Distribution
Printed in the U.S.A.

Urban Press
P.O. Box 8881
Pittsburgh, PA 15221-0881
412.646.2780

Table of Contents

Introduction		v
week 1	New Perspectives on Purpose	1
week 2	I Found Mine in a Book	4
week 3	Panning For Gold	7
week 4	What's in a Name?	10
week 5	Fruit and Purpose	12
week 6	Who Are You, Really?	14
week 7	Be Encouraged	16
week 8	That's Absurd!	19
week 9	The World is Waiting	21
week 10	Childhood Clues	23
week 11	Filled With the Spirit	25
week 12	The Music of the Future	27
week 13	Are You Happy?	29
week 14	What Options Do You Have?	31
week 15	The Pieces of Your Past	33
week 16	We Can't Do It Until We Know It	35
week 17	Why Are You Doing It?	37
week 18	Free To Be Me	39
week 19	Permission To Be Creative	41
week 20	The Jonah Complex	43
week 21	Yes and No	45
week 22	A Letter From Jacquie	47
week 23	What Do You Fear?	49
week 24	What You Do Isn't Who You Are	51
week 25	Dealing With Discouragement	53
week 26	For God, In God	55
week 27	What Makes You Cry?	57
week 28	Children, Parents, and Purpose	59
week 29	Knowing the Will of God	62
week 30	Toxic Relationships	64
week 31	Nancy's Story	66
week 32	Opposition	69
week 33	Enjoy Your Work	71

week 34	Flavored Water	73
week 35	Courage	75
week 36	Small is Good	77
week 37	Purpose Pain	79
week 38	Never Too Young	81
week 39	God Wants More	83
week 40	Just and Only	86
week 41	Handling Criticism	89
week 42	He Changed the "S" to "P"	92
week 43	Stop Trying to Figure It Out	94
week 44	Moses: "Here I Am"	96
week 45	Moses: "Who Am I?"	98
week 46	Moses: "Who Sent Me?"	100
week 47	Moses: "What If I Fail?"	102
week 48	Moses: "Just a Staff"	104
week 49	Moses: Excuses, Excuses	106
week 50	Moses: Into the Game	108
week 51	Celebrate a Failure	110
week 52	Hit It Hard and Wish It Well	112
	End Notes	114

Introduction

This book began in March 2001 with an idea. We were planning the launch of my website, www.purposequest.com, and I wanted to do something different. So many sites were boring or at least didn't have new material that encouraged people to return. I didn't want that to happen with mine, so I thought about what I could do to create traffic to my site.

At the same time, I had received many requests from people who attended my purpose teaching sessions over the years. They all said the same thing: "We need to hear from you more often. Can we write you? We need ongoing help if we are going to discover and clarify our purpose."

With that in mind, I decided to do a weekly email called *The Monday Memo*. My objectives were simple. I wanted to show up every Monday and ask people, "Do you know your purpose? Are you having faith for your time? What steps are taking now to make your dreams come true?" *The Monday Memo* would also serve to remind people that there were more materials and products on the website that would help them be more purposeful and productive.

The first *Monday Memo* was sent to about 30 people; the rest is history. The *Memo* currently has thousands of subscribers all around the world. Every Monday I delight in the letters and feedback I receive from many people whom I've never met and may never meet. Here's an example of how *The Monday Memo* helped one African reader:

> I am saying this from the bottom of my heart that you are such a blessing. Ever since I started receiving your Memos, your teaching in this area has

been more than helpful. It makes me take a close look into my life to see what I was born to do. Even though I haven't fully discovered what my purpose is, I find my faith has increased, and I am more confident that it is about to unfold. So many things have happened and I know that God is preparing for this discovery. It's my prayer that your soul may prosper as your spirit prospers. With courage you are reaching out to people in many nations by imparting such a huge gift with a willing heart. May the God bless you and give you grace. – *Sam*

One year after I began *The Monday Memo*, I started to distribute weekly Bible studies, and today more than 3,500 receive them. What has all that got to do with this book? I decided that if people can benefit from *The Monday Memo* and Bible studies through email, then why not publish some of the best of them in book form? With that in mind, I present to you this volume entitled, *Unlocking the Power of Your Purpose.*

Included are 52 *Monday Memos* that have been adapted and edited. I present them in random order so you can open the book and begin anywhere. You may see some topics covered more than once, but I trust that when you do, there will be some fresh insight to help you clarify your purpose. Throughout this volume, I use the term PurposeQuest™ regularly. I define the PurposeQuest *as your journey that enables you to clarify and fulfill your purpose.*

I've taught audiences about purpose since 1991. I've also counseled thousands around the world to help them clarify their purpose. Everything I do is predicated on one basic principle: *If God wants you to do His will—and He does—then He must reveal to you what His will is.* The Lord can't hold you accountable for what you don't know.

At the end of this volume, there's information that will enable you to enroll for *The Monday Memo*. I hope that these studies whet your appetite for more. The PurposeQuest is a lifelong process, and we need to be in touch to encourage one another along the way. Feel free to write me and share your own

PurposeQuest stories. Who knows, your story may find its way into a future volume! So are you ready to get started? As you begin this book, I pray the following prayer for you:

> I pray also that the eyes of your heart may be enlightened in order that you may know the hope to which he has called you, the riches of his glorious inheritance in the saints, and his incomparably great power for us who believe (Ephesians 1:18-19).

John W. Stanko
Pittsburgh, Pennsylvania USA
July 2015

WEEK #1

New Perspectives on Purpose

I receive a lot of questions when I lecture on the topic of purpose. Over the years, the questions asked most often, along with my answers, have been as follows:

Q. Can my purpose change over time?

A. No. How you fulfill your purpose may change, but your purpose remains the same. I have fulfilled my purpose, which is to create order out of chaos in a number of different job roles. My purpose is the same; how I do it may change.

Q. Can I have more than one purpose?

A. No. You can have many gifts and talents, or different ways to express or fulfill your purpose, but your purpose is a clear, simple, and singular summary of your essence.

Q. Should or is it possible for a husband and wife to have the same purpose?

A. No. While it is possible for a couple to have the same purpose, I have found it to be rare. Even if both work in the same business, mission or ministry, each partner will have a different purpose and function in that same organization. Usually, those purposes complement one another.

Q. What is the difference between a gift and purpose?

A. A gift is like a tool that you carry with you to help fulfill your purpose. A plumber's purpose is not to "wrench." The wrench helps the plumber achieve his or her purpose to repair or build. Your gifts do the same for you, but they are not to be confused with your purpose.

Q. What is the difference between ministry and purpose?

A. Too often, we are tempted to separate what we do in

church from what we do outside of church. We tend to think of ministry as related to church work, and purpose as something that may or may not fit into our church role. I contend that there is no difference between the two.

I met with a man in Atlanta who had a career in human resources. It was clear to me, however, that he was functioning as a pastor to many people. When I suggested that perhaps he was a chaplain or pastor in his company, he rejected the idea at first because he didn't have a pulpit or even enjoy public speaking. Yet he had clearly cared for and been a shepherd to people during his entire corporate career.

By the end of our meeting, he began to see his purpose was to care for people in a business setting. He saw that his purpose was his ministry; it just wasn't taking place within the walls of a church building. That knowledge set him free to be who God made him to be and freed him from thinking his ministry and purpose were two different things.

Perhaps you aren't clear about your purpose because you have put God in a box. Maybe you are a prophet, but everyone knows that prophets only function in a church setting. Who said that? You bring healing and wholeness to people, but never lay hands on anyone or do it within a church. Does that limit your purpose or usefulness to God? Are you a preacher, but your pulpit is in a school or hospital? I met a man once whose title was school principal or headmaster, but whose purpose was to pastor the children who attended his school, and to pastor their parents as well.

The following words of Robert K. Greenleaf can help set you free to minister (which simply means to serve) in whatever setting the Lord chooses for you, whether it's inside or outside the church:

> The great religious prophets of the future will not necessarily be theologians, philosophers, or people of literature. They are as likely to be lawyers, doctors, businesspeople, scientists, or politicians, and they will carry out their prophetic roles while

functioning at a high level of excellence in their professional field. In fact, unless significant prophecy emerges in all of these places, the vision, without which the people perish, will not be sufficiently evident.

The world society in which we are all inextricably involved is far too complex, it is in too revolutionary a mood, and it is fast becoming too literate and aware of its sources of expertise for very much of the prophetic wisdom it needs to be uttered by ministers, scholars, or writers. These people will, of course, continue to serve, but more on a par with those who are more immersed in the ongoing work of the world.

Businesses, government bureaus, law firms, clinics, and scientific laboratories have not only become large, sophisticated institutions and important sources of new knowledge, but are just as likely to harbor a philosopher, a prophet, or a saint as is the monastery or the university.[1]

Week #2

I Found Mine in a Book

I once met a man named Michael who had read all my books. The church he attended was started in part because the founders had read my purpose message. At the time of our meeting, Michael was working for the church. When I asked him what his purpose was, he said, "I'm not sure." So I did what I always do: I began asking questions.

It didn't take long for me to hear some key words: music, excellence, and projects were a few of them. Then one phrase stood out. He said, "I like to make things sing." What a colorful phrase! He wasn't saying that everything had to be musical, though. "Making everything sing" stated his commitment to excellence in whatever he did. He didn't want things to "hum" or "whistle;" he wanted every project, whether musical or not, to be the best expression of its unique purpose. I left Michael to consider whether or not his life purpose is to make things sing.

I receive many inquiries from people needing help finding their purpose. It recently occurred to me that I found my purpose—to create order out of chaos—when I had read those words in a book. They "jumped out" at me, and I have never been the same since. I thought I would provide some phrases for you to study to see if the same thing would happen to you.

I found the list below in a book entitled, *Whistle While You Work: Heeding Your Life's Calling*, by Richard Leider and David A. Shapiro. The authors refer to this as a list of "Calling Cards"—a concept they developed to help people like you and me find our life's calling and purpose. They explain:

Each of these callings describes a core gift. Each calling comes directly from someone's experience. We have been collecting callings in seminars, workshops, and coaching sessions with individuals and groups from all walks of life. The list of 52 callings we have come up with represents the "essence of essences" in our research. (This doesn't mean that there are not callings other than our 52; it does, however, mean that these 52 represent those that have best withstood real-world testing.)[2]

I am including half of their list in this study; you will find the other half in the following one. Read both lists and see if anything stirs you. Feel free to focus on one of these phrases that seems to be a close description of who you are. Allow God to "energize" that statement and make it your own, or modify it in some way to make it a better fit for you. I hope the Lord will do for you what He did for me: by taking someone else's words, I was able to define my purpose. I hope that you are able to do the same thing. Happy seeking!

List of Calling Cards

Category One: Realistic
Building Things
Fixing Things
Growing Things
Making Things Work
Shaping Environments
Solving Problems

Category Two: Conventional
Straightening Things Up
Doing the Numbers
Getting Things Right
Operating Things
Organizing Things
Processing Things

Category Three: Investigative
Advancing Ideas
Investigating Things
Analyzing Information
Researching Things
Putting the Pieces Together
Translating Things
Getting to the Heart of Matters

WEEK #3
Panning for Gold

I suppose that if I had lived in Alaska, my first book would have been titled, *Life is a Gold Mine: Can You Pan It?* as opposed to *Can You Dig It?* The early Alaskan settlers panned for gold in Alaska's streams and rivers in hopes of finding their golden treasure. With that in mind, I decided to try my hand at gold panning one time while on an Alaskan cruise.

I did indeed find about ten small pieces of gold during my panning experience. Digging or panning for gold is similar to what you and I go through to find our life purpose. How so? consider these similarities:

1. *You can pan on your own, but having someone who knows how to do it is a great help.* My guide Tom had begun panning two years earlier. He taught us the proper procedures that enabled each one of us to find gold. When you are looking for your purpose, it often helps to involve other people. Ask them what they think your purpose may be. Better yet, find someone who knows their purpose and ask them to help you find yours.

2. *Panning is hard work.* As I stood over a trough, panning for the gold I found, my back began to ache. I thought about those who panned in the cold Alaskan weather, standing in cold water, and bending over for most of the day. Finding your purpose can be hard work, too, and there is no guarantee when you'll find it or what you'll go through to discover the big golden nugget awaiting you.

3. *You don't need a lot of tools.* You only need a pan to discover gold, not a lot of sophisticated equipment. As you search for your purpose, you start where you are, with what

you have, and look around you in faith.

4. *You can't see the gold right away.* When I began, my pan was filled with dirt and gravel. When you search for your purpose; you can't see the "gold" because of all the other "stuff" in your life. It's there, however, and you simply have to know how to find it. *It's exciting when you find the gold.* When I found the gold at the bottom of my pan, I felt like I was rich! When you find your life purpose, you feel the same way. The God of the universe knows who you are and He gave you something to do that's just right for you.

5. *The gold stays in the pan.* Gold is so heavy that it's almost impossible to lose it when you're panning. Your life purpose is the same way; it's a part of you that goes with you wherever you are and is relevant no matter what mistakes you've made.

In the previous study, I promised to give you the second half of the "Calling Cards" from the book entitled, *Whistle While You Work: Heeding Your Life's Calling,* by Richard Leider and David A. Shapiro.[3]

So are you ready to pan for gold? Put these calling cards in your pan and swirl them around to see if any stay in the bottom as the gold of your life. If you're not sure, then keep swirling them around in your mind and heart. Keep looking, and I promise that you'll find the riches that lie in all the "stuff" in your life.

Category Four: Enterprising
Bringing Out Potential
Exploring the Way
Managing Things
Persuading People
Starting Things
Selling Intangibles
Opening Doors
Empowering Others

Category Five: Social
Awakening Spirit
Bringing Joy
Building Relationships
Creating Dialogue
Creating Trust
Facilitating Change
Getting Participation
Giving Care
Healing Wounds
Helping Overcome Obstacles
Instructing People
Resolving Disputes

Category Six: Artistic
Adding Humor
Breaking Molds
Creating Things
Composing Things
Designing Things
Moving Through Space
Performing Events
Seeing Possibilities
Seeing the Big Picture
Writing Things

WEEK #4

What's in a Name?

My encounter with Dennis is one of my favorite PurposeQuest stories. Dennis attended a seminar in Virginia a few years ago and was not impressed with my message. In fact, he politely but firmly opposed it as a "management fad" that was not to be found in the Bible. I urged him to be patient until I reached the end of the seminar, but he found it hard to do so. He just wasn't buying what I said.

After the session, Dennis came to me and reiterated his disagreement with my conclusions. He felt that my purpose message was too subjective and open to misinterpretation. He then issued his plea: "I challenge you to find any theme of purpose in the diverse activities I have been involved with in my lifetime." Intrigued by his challenge, I accepted.

As he went through his list of seemingly unrelated activities, I started to regret that I had agreed to the challenge. Then I saw something that gave me hope. "It seems to me," I said, "that the common theme here is not *what* you've done, but *why* you've done it. Isn't it true that you've been called on to do all those things because they weren't quite what they could be?" I closed with the statement, "It seems to me that you were born to bring a measure of excellence to whatever the Lord wants you to do."

Dennis still wasn't impressed and left, only to return the next day for the rest of my seminar. This time he shared an exciting revelation he had the night before. He told the class that after he left the previous meeting, he had been reminded of the literal meaning of his name "Dennis" in Greek. Dennis means "discerner of excellence," and this man had suddenly come face-to-face with a very dramatic understanding of who he was and what he was born to do.

I wish all PurposeQuests ended so well and neatly, but they don't. Some people search and search and become discouraged in the process. Others settle for half answers, and still others for pat answers that lack personal meaning and application. Where do you fit in?

I want to suggest a few more guidelines for finding your purpose. Consider these issues if you are still searching or helping someone who is.

1. *Your purpose may not be found in what you're doing, but rather in why you're doing it.* That was the case with Dennis. He brought excellence to non-excellent performance by doing many different things. In trying to find his purpose, he was focusing on the wrong thing.

2. *Your purpose may be defined by who you're not.* You will often go where you are least comfortable in order to fulfill your purpose. My purpose is to create order out of chaos. I love order but always find myself, at least for a while, in chaos. The very thing I'm not—chaotic—gives expression to the very thing I am—ordered.

3. *Your purpose may be expressed in many different ways.* I create order out of chaos, but I've done it as a writer, pastor, consultant, teacher, and administrator. I've been involved in many activities, but there has always been one common purpose and theme.

4. *Often your purpose is as close as the name your parents gave you,* only you can't see it. God can open your eyes, however, to see what you couldn't previously see. I trust that this will soon be the experience either for you or someone you're helping. Are there any clues in your name or nickname that can help you find your purpose?

WEEK #5

Fruit and Purpose

I've never looked for a job in my life. Every job I've had has come looking for me. And each job has needed what I had to offer: a life purpose of creating order out of chaos and potential.

As I was sitting on the beach one day in Hilton Head Island, South Carolina, I was thinking about what Jesus said: "By their fruit you will know them." What fruit or results are you known for? If you can answer that, you're well on your way to knowing your life purpose.

I'm known as someone who can bring order out of a mess. I see the potential in people and situations that others can't see. It's not what I hope to do or produce. It's the fruit that I was born to produce; it's the real me.

A friend sent me an article entitled, "Are You Listening to Your Life?" by Parker Palmer. I want to quote it to help you "listen" for the fruit that you're known for:

> Vocation doesn't come from a voice "out there" calling me to become something I'm not. It comes from a voice "in here" calling me to be the person I was born to be.
>
> Accepting this birthright gift of self turns out to be even more demanding than attempting to become someone else. I've sometimes responded to that demand by ignoring the gift or hiding or fleeing from it, and I don't think I'm alone. A Hasidic tale reveals both the universal tendency to want to be someone else and the importance of becoming one's self. Rabbi Zusya, when he was an old

man, said, "In the coming world, they will not ask me, 'Why were you not Moses?' They will ask me, "Why were you not Zusya?'"

When we lose track of true self, how can we pick up the trail? Our lives speak through our actions and reactions, our intuitions and instincts, our feelings and bodily states, perhaps more profoundly than through words. If we can learn to read our own responses, we'll receive the guidance we need to live more authentic lives. The soul speaks only under quiet, inviting, and safe conditions. If we take some time to sit silently listening, the soul will tell us the truth about ourselves—the full, messy truth. An often ignored dimension of the quest for wholeness is the need to embrace what we dislike about ourselves as well as what we're proud of, our liabilities as well as our strengths.

Are you in a job or life situation where you can bear the fruit that was meant to come from you? If not, what are you willing to do to make that happen? If you are doing what you do solely for money or security—no matter how nobly or spiritually—you are a hireling, a hired hand that may very well be cut off from who you are and what is important to you. If that's the case, then there is no way you will be known by the fruit you were created to bear because you aren't bearing any.

I urge you to listen in the quiet of your own heart to identify your fruit and then take steps to be in a place to bear fruit. After all, you won't ever be asked, "Why weren't you Moses or Paul?" but what will you answer if asked, "Did you bear the fruit that you were meant to produce?"

WEEK #6

Who Are You, Really?

It's a sad sight to see, although I encounter it every week—people who are in situations that are going nowhere, hoping that somehow their circumstances will change. Others are hoping that they themselves will change and suddenly become someone they have never been. Usually, they will quote Philippians 4:13, which states, "I can do all things through Him [Christ] who strengthens me."

Most of the time, I don't have the heart to tell them that their interpretation of Philippians 4:13 isn't correct. You *can't* be anything you want to be, nor will God change you into someone He never intended you to be in the first place. The context of Philippians 4:13 is about finances. Paul was saying he had learned to be content with a lot or a little; he had learned to be happy with what God provided at any point in time.

Anyone who is trying to be who God didn't intend for them to be is trying to do something in their own strength, not in God's strength. For example, I tried for years to be a pastor, yet no amount of trying or hiding behind Philippians 4:13 could make me a pastor. In the end, I had to face the fact that God didn't create me to be a pastor. He created me to be who I am.

So who are you? To find out, perhaps you must first admit that you are not who you are trying to be. Maybe you have taken on a role that you always desired or accepted a position that others have given you. At this point, you may have to face the reality that what you're doing isn't working, that in a sense God has withheld His favor and blessing because you are not in the right place, doing the right thing. Only then, when you've accepted who you aren't, can God show you who you are.

God wants you to know your purpose. He will not empower you to be who you are not, but He will empower you to be the fullest, greatest expression of who you are. In that setting, you will be able to do all things because God is with you in reality. You will not be guilty of wishful thinking.

If I could personally do one thing for you right now, I would release you from trying to be who you are not. I would tell you that you haven't failed; it's just time for you to move on. Furthermore, I would look you in the eye and say, "You *can't* do all things, but you *can* do the things that God wants you to do. So stop pretending and move on. God is with you."

May you find the path where God can truly enable you to do great things for Him and other people. In other words, I hope you find the real you.

Week #7

Be Encouraged

If I asked you what your purpose in life is, what would you say? Would you be able to give me a clear, simple set of words that describes who you are, or would you respond with a phrase that sounds nice, but doesn't really get to the heart of your existence?

While doing research for my book, *I Wrote This Book On Purpose . . . So You Can Know Yours,* I discovered author Laurence Boldt. In the introduction to his book, Boldt wrote:

> The quest for the work you love—it all begins with the two simple questions: Who am I? And What in the world am I doing here? While as old as humanity itself, these perennial questions are born anew in every man and woman who is privileged to walk upon this earth. Every sane man and woman, at some point in his or her life, is confronted by these questions—some while but children; more in adolescence and youth; still more at midlife or when facing retirement; and even the toughest customers at the death of a loved one or when they themselves have a brush with death. Yes, somewhere, sometime, we all find ourselves face-to-face with the questions, Who am I? And What am I here for?
>
> And we do make some attempt to answer them. We ask our parents and teachers, and it seems they do not know. They refer us to political and religious institutions, which often crank out canned answers devoid of personal meaning. Some even tell us that

life has no meaning, save for eating and breeding. Most of us are smart enough to recognize that canned answers or begging the question will not do. We must find real answers for ourselves. But that takes more heart and effort than we are often willing to give.[4]

Finding your purpose can be hard work, but it is well worth the effort. Your purpose not only gives you peace and a sense of destiny but also the energy and focus that will enable you to make a difference in your world. Boldt goes on to write:

> Failing to find the work you love has costs, not only to your self-esteem, relationships, health, and creativity, but to your world. As a human community, we all lose when people's creative abilities do not find expression in constructive, purposeful action. We lose in terms of needless human suffering and untapped human potential. Around the globe, useless, even degrading work steals the spirit and saps the joy from the lives of millions, while much necessary work goes undone. Giving your gifts benefits the world, not only through the direct contributions you make and the joy you radiate, but through the living example you provide others of what is possible for them. Determine to play your part in creating the kind of world you want to live in.[5]

If you are still searching for your purpose, don't give up. Keep digging; keep panning; God will reward your efforts. I can't tell you when, but I promise the search will be worth it.

If you know your purpose, I want to point out one sentence from the above quote: "Around the globe, useless, even degrading work steals the spirit and saps the joy from the lives of millions, while much necessary work goes undone." Are you neglecting "necessary work" because you are giving yourself to things not related to your life purpose? If that is the case, what are you prepared to do about it?

If I can help you in your search, don't hesitate to go to www.purposequest.com, where I have posted more material to assist you. Or write me, for often I have been able to help people see what was right before them all along—their life purpose. Do what you can now to clarify and fulfill your purpose. The world is waiting for you to be clear.

WEEK #8
That's Absurd!

I always receive a lot of mail after I send my weekly email newsletter, *The Monday Memo*. Most of the time people write because they are having trouble coming to grips with discovering their specific purpose.

While I always share tips or techniques that may help you find your purpose, most often finding it comes down to hearing the voice of God. It involves recognizing that still, small voice that doesn't shout over the other voices vying for your attention. The still, small voice simply waits for you and me to stifle all the rival voices that can distract us and then quietly communicates with us.

Recently, I was reading a book by Henri Nouwen called *Making All Things New*. Nouwen wrote in it:

> From all that I said about our worried, over-filled lives, it is clear that we are usually surrounded by so much inner and outer noise that it is hard to truly hear our God when he is speaking to us. We have often become deaf, unable to know when God calls us and unable to understand in which direction he calls us. Thus, our lives have become absurd. In the word absurd we find the Latin word *surdus*, which means "deaf." A spiritual life requires discipline because we need to learn to listen to God, who constantly speaks but whom we seldom hear. When, however, we learn to listen, our lives become obedient lives. The word obedient comes from the Latin word *audire*, which means "listening." A spiritual discipline is necessary in order to move

slowly from an absurd to an obedient life, from a life filled with noisy worries to a life in which there is some free inner space where we can listen to our God and follow his guidance.[6]

A life without purpose truly is an absurd life. Determine to discipline yourself to drown out or reduce the noise in your life so you can hear God. Spend some time praying and have faith that you will hear His voice. Be prepared with a pen and paper to write down what you think you hear Him say. After all, if God wants you to do His will, He will tell you what that will is. If you are to be a person of purpose, you must live an obedient life that follows the directions you hear from God. I trust and pray that you can hear Him and then obey what you hear. It really is the only way to live.

WEEK #9

The World Is Waiting

In a recent letter I received, someone wrote:

> Dear Doc,
>
> If only you knew what it is that you've done for me. In an age when the Internet is being used for so many horrible things...you're there.
>
> Thanks.
>
> Gideon

I include this not to draw attention to what I've done, but to encourage you to do what you are yet to do. When I started *The Monday Memo* a few years ago, I had no idea how popular it would become or how God would use it to impact and direct so many lives. You never know how God will use something that you do until after you do it. You can plan and hope, dream and execute, but there is still that unexpected, unknown element that can surprise or disappoint you. The bottom line is: You have to give God something to bless before He can bless it.

There was a young boy in Jesus' day who gave Jesus his lunch of five loaves of bread and two fish. Jesus took that lunch, blessed it, and distributed it to thousands. It was just a simple lunch, but in God's hands it fed a multitude with plenty left over. You need to stop focusing on how little you have in your hands and start seeing how you can get that little bit into God's hands so He can multiply it. In your hands, all you will have is stale bread and smelly fish. In God's hands, however, you may have a feast that can satisfy many others and still provide for you. The choice is yours: Hold onto what you have until it's perfect or release it now and see what happens.

You don't know what God will do with the poem you write, the song you compose, the book you write, the business you start, the class you take, or the trip you take. That's why your goals for this year are so important. If you haven't done so already, why not write down at least three specific things that you would like to accomplish in the next few months. Share these three things with someone you love and trust who can hold you accountable to get them done and will rejoice with you when they are finished. Write down not only what you will do, but also the time frame in which you will have it done. Don't try to overanalyze what to do or how to do it. Just get it out there and see how God will use it.

I believe that there are many more ideas in you, just like *The Monday Memo,* waiting to burst onto the world scene. I can't promise that you'll change the world with what you do, but I can promise that you'll change *your* world. You'll never be the same, and the joy of achievement will spur you on to even greater things. The world is waiting for what's in you; don't keep it waiting any longer.

WEEK #10

Childhood Clues

I have visited South Africa 30 times, and I always look forward to going there. In fact, I've traveled almost 3 million miles, and I'm still excited to get on a plane and go anywhere. I had a friend who said he enjoyed taking me to the airport because he could feel my energy level rising when we were on the way there. Recently another friend asked me, "Do you still enjoy all the travel?" I replied that I do not simply enjoy it or like it, I am exhilarated by it!

My family never traveled while I was growing up, nor did we ever take a family vacation. One evening when I was about ten years old, my father took me in the car for a ride. We ended up at the Pittsburgh Airport where we spent the evening watching planes land and take off. The airport had stores, a game room, a movie theater, and an observation deck where you paid ten cents to go out on the deck and watch the planes. That was more than 50 years ago, but I can still remember the sense of excitement I had hearing the engines starting up and seeing the power of a plane during takeoff. That night, as young as I was, I vowed to go back to the airport many times when I grew up, and I have made good on my vow.

Travel is an important part of who I am and what I do. God used that childhood airport visit to put something in me that won't go away. Some childhood experiences are positive and some negative, but they all play a role in shaping who we become. Very often, there are clues to our life purpose that come early in life. Recapturing those memories can play an important role in defining your purpose.

Consider childhood stories of the following people:

As a child in England, he spent hours creating cardboard sets for his puppet shows to entertain his family.—Andrew Lloyd Webber, producer of the theatrical rendition of *Phantom of the Opera.*

Cut from his basketball team as a youngster, he still dreamed of playing basketball one day.—Michael Jordan, the world's greatest player.

Swimming to gain strength in his two broken arms, this teenager changed dreams from becoming an astronaut to aquanaut.—Jacques Cousteau, famous underwater explorer.

This young boy was fascinated with anatomical diagrams in the *World Book Encyclopedia.*—Jonas Salk, who developed the polio vaccine.

This college dropout had ideas about information access.—Bill Gates, founder of Microsoft and the world's richest man.

What was your favorite game as a child? What did you spend time daydreaming about? What did you do as a child that made you the happiest? What positive or negative experiences led you to make a life-shaping decision that is still with you today? Have you lost contact with some part of your youth that could once again provide you with purpose and excitement?

As you search your past, you may find keys to the present that will unlock your future. Why not spend some time thinking about your childhood with a writing tablet in front of you? Write down what you remember and see if there are any childhood clues that emerge to help you define your purpose. You may have an experience similar to my airport visit that can reshape your adult life if you let it.

WEEK #11
Filled With the Spirit

I was thinking about a man in the Bible named Bezalel. It is said about this man that he was "filled with the Spirit of God." Now, I don't know about you, but when I see or hear that phrase, I assume that the person who is "filled" is probably a holy man, preacher, or saint. Surely, he was "filled with the Spirit" to perform miracles, preach, or fulfill some other religious activity. With Bezalel, however, this was not the case.

> Then the Lord said to Moses, "See, I have chosen Bezalel son of Uri, the son of Hur, of the tribe of Judah, and I have filled him with the Spirit of God, with skill, ability and knowledge in all kinds of crafts—to make artistic designs for work in gold, silver and bronze, to cut and set stones, to work in wood, and to engage in all kinds of craftsmanship" (Exodus 31:1-5).

Bezalel wasn't full of the Spirit to do religious things; he was full of the Spirit to work with his hands and create artistic masterpieces. He was an exceptional craftsman, which was the will of God for Bezalel's life. God gave him special ability and gave him His "Spirit" to excel in the area of creativity.

When searching for our God-given purpose, too often we limit the search to activities normally associated with church work. We may not think that the "Spirit" may be on us to write, teach a class, paint, sing opera, run a business, or lead a government agency. The passage above let's us know that life purpose isn't restricted to church work. Your purpose may take you to places you didn't previously consider to be part of God's purpose for you.

Do you like to work with your hands? Can you fix or create things? Do you have an eye for beauty, color, or symmetry? Then why can't some expression of those things be your life purpose? You don't have to preach or counsel to do God's will. You can create beautiful things that bring pleasure to God and others and be in the center of God's will for your life.

What are you "filled with the Spirit" to do? Don't see that as a hobby, and don't wait until you can do something more "spiritual" before you feel you're doing the will of God. It's time for the painters to paint, the poets to rhyme, the singers to sing, the writers to write, the conductors to conduct, and the dancers to dance. If we can find people who are "filled with the Spirit" to do those things, the world will be a better place and God's will shall be done.

WEEK #12
The Music of the Future

Every once in a while, I run into a quote and desperately wish I had said it myself because it's so powerful. I heard one of those quotes one morning in church, looked at my wife, and said, "I've got to write about that!" To the best of my research, this quote can be attributed to "Captain" Bob Smith, a motivational speaker and it goes like this: "Hope is hearing the music of the future. Faith is dancing to it today!"

Both clarifying your purpose and setting goals involve hearing the music of the future. You look beyond where you are and what you're doing to see yourself from God's perspective. You see yourself doing what you were born to do and achieving what you are here to achieve, even though you're not at that place yet. As you read this study, aren't you really listening for a certain sound that provides clarity and direction? When you hear it, you will begin to tap your foot, and before you know it, you will be dancing to a tune that no one else can hear.

Once you see your purpose or visualize a goal, you need to have faith to walk it out in everyday life. In other words, you should begin to dance to the music of the future by preparing yourself in faith to be the greatest expression of your purpose that you can be. You can take intermediate steps today that will help you reach your goal tomorrow.

Please open your ears and heart to hear the sound of your life music. It may be a faint sound or only one musical phrase, but it's playing. Have hope that God will let you hear some of that music now. Then, when you hear the music, have faith! Take some steps that will prepare you to achieve your destiny and fulfill your life purpose.

"Hope is hearing the music of the future. Faith is dancing to it today!" I trust you will hear the music of the future and not just the monotonous sounds of the past and present. I hope you will catch a glimpse of what you can be and not just see what you've been. If you've been dancing with your present self, I encourage you to change partners and dance with the you of the future. You need to get acquainted, this present and future you, and as a team, you will both do great things.

WEEK #13
Are You Happy?

Are you happy? I didn't ask if you were reasonably satisfied. I asked if you are happy. I'm not sure you can say you're happy just because you aren't sad. Do you have enthusiasm for what you do? Is there a joy in your heart and life that energizes you? If not, what price are you willing to pay to get in touch with that level of happiness?

Several years ago, I asked myself that question, and the answer was, "No!" One day, I found myself sitting on a plane and began a conversation with the man next to me. He was going to a convention to make a speech, which is what he did for a living. He had written a book entitled, *If Aristotle Ran General Motors*, and made a good living talking about his book to business people. As he was sharing with me what he did, I said to myself, "That's what I want to do!" I didn't want to talk about Aristotle to business people, but I did want to travel and speak about my passion in front of anyone who would listen. I wasn't happy doing what I was doing then—it was time to do something else.

Joy is a barometer, an indicator that tells you if you are on course in your life and career. If you're doing what you do and have money as your main or perhaps only motivation, then you are a "hireling," renting out your skills to the highest bidder. If you have the money but not the joy, you are missing the main fuel for creativity, meaning, and fulfillment. If your joy is gone and you're unhappy, that may be reason enough to begin considering your options. Do you want to spend the rest of your life feeling like you do now?

I am not suggesting we worship at the altar of

happiness as a life purpose. Joy is an important indication you are functioning in your purpose, but that doesn't mean you won't have troubles and challenges. The joy is there to carry you through those tough times. Nehemiah said it when he exhorted the people, "The joy of the Lord is your strength" (Nehemiah 8:10). If you aren't happy, you may not have the strength you need to fulfill your purpose. In fact, if you aren't happy, you may not be in your purpose at all.

I was asked at a church seminar one time, "Dr. Stanko, where is the cross in what you teach?" The woman had a legitimate question. Was I promoting a selfish pursuit of personal pleasure and hiding it behind what I called "doing the will of God" in fulfilling our purpose? I answered by referring to the Apostle Paul, a man of purpose.

Paul's purpose was to preach the gospel to the Gentiles, which is where he had his greatest success. There was plenty of "cross" in Paul's purpose. Just read Second Corinthians, chapters four and eleven, to see what hardship he endured and pressure he was under. Yet the joy of his purpose carried him through all those things, and later he wrote, "I have fought the good fight, I have finished the race, I have kept the faith" (2 Timothy 4:7). His joy empowered him to finish.

In regard to my own purpose, I love creating order out of chaos but, if the truth be known, doing it in church settings isn't always my favorite work. Yet it's the will of God for me. When I bring order, I feel His joy and presence, but the cross is present as well. Jesus, for the joy set before Him, endured His cross and despised His shame (see Hebrews 12:1-2). He couldn't deny or refuse His joy; for anyone to do so would make the trials of life an almost intolerable burden.

What about you? Are you cut off from your joy? Are you happy? Meditate on these questions and see what answers you come up with. I hope you will answer honestly and set your heart to do whatever it takes to reconnect your life with your joy.

WEEK #14

What Options Do You Have?

I receive a lot of feedback from people who are "stuck" in jobs that aren't related to their life purpose. "What do we do with our years of seniority and assurance of a decent salary, when we don't feel connected to our purpose?" Let me answer this question by making a few points:

1. *Know your purpose.* Most people who can't see how to get out of their current job usually don't have a clear, concise purpose statement. It's hard to see how you can move on until you have a vision of where you're going. Recently, I was talking with a woman who was working for a bank, although she loved to improve women's self-esteem through all kinds of practical training. She also enjoyed doing hair, nails, and other beauty-related activities. Our entire conversation focused on what her life purpose was. Because she went away clear about her purpose when we ended our conversation, she had ideas of what she could do after her bank job (where she was encountering many problems).

2. *Choose wisely.* It is important that you choose jobs that are best suited for you and your talents whenever possible. Stephen Covey warns not to start climbing a ladder until you're sure it's leaning against the right wall! If at all possible, don't take a job simply because it's offered to you. Ask yourself whether or not the job or career has the potential to release you to growth and joy. If it doesn't, then don't take it. If you do, you may be writing me in five years asking how you can get out! That is tough to do, for the financial obligations at that point may necessitate that you stay put, even though you're not content.

3. *Work hard.* I know that you already work hard, but when you know your purpose, your real work may begin at 5:00 p.m. when you end your day job and are finally free to embrace your purpose. For years, I wrote, taught, and studied studied after my regular work day was over. I spent time preparing for the day when I would be released to speak and consult. I developed expertise on my jobs that would add to the repertoire of services I could eventually offer. The woman I mentioned above is probably going to have to go to night school to get the certification she needs to fulfill her purpose. Many times there is no way around making that sacrifice.

It occurred to me this past week that Jesus was a carpenter and Paul made tents, but neither man ever talked about their trade. In both cases, someone else told us about their occupations. Certainly Paul never mentioned what he did for a living. Yet in every letter he wrote, Paul talked about his purpose of bringing the gospel to the Gentiles. He talked about his life, not in terms of what he did to make money, but in terms of what he did to change the world. You must begin to define yourself not in terms of what you are doing but in terms of who you are at the core of your being. That's where your purpose resides.

If you are "stuck," first tell me what your purpose is. From there, what steps can you take to fulfill it, even if it is only part-time or on weekends? It may not be much, but for now it's the best option. Don't wait until next week to do something about this situation; do it now. It is said that every journey starts with the first step. Take your first step now by reading a book, enrolling for a class, setting aside two nights for your second business, or beginning to research a new career in earnest. Start making your way out of your dead end road and see if you can't find the highway of purpose.

WEEK #15

The Pieces of Your Past

I try to read a book every month that focuses on the topics of purpose and productivity. One such book I recently read was *Forgetting Ourselves on Purpose* by Brian Mahan. In the book, Mahan describes a childhood experience of Dorothy Day, founder of the Catholic Worker Movement on the Lower East Side of New York City. As I have mentioned in the past, childhood dreams, failures, and goals can hold clues to help you find your purpose. Mahan quotes Day's own words:

> I think my "pilgrimage" began when I was a child, when I was seven or eight . . . I'm sitting with my mother, and she's telling me about some trouble in the world, about children like me who don't have enough food—they're dying. I'm eating a doughnut, I think. I ask my mother why other children don't have doughnuts and I do . . . I don't remember her words, but I can still see her face; it's the face of someone who is sad, and resigned. . . Most of all, I remember trying to understand what it meant—me eating a doughnut, and lots of children with no food at all. . . . I don't remember my words, I just remember holding the doughnut up and hoping she'd take it and give it to someone, some child . . . . I didn't eat that doughnut! I put it down on the kitchen table. . . . I asked her if God knew someone nearby, or if He could help us with our modest doughnut plan. . . . I don't remember asking her that, asking her how we might enlist God in this effort; but she says I kept talking about God and

Jesus and feeding the hungry with doughnuts, until she told me, please, to stop![7]

Here was an adult woman immersed in something significant for the poor and the signs of her purpose first became clear in a childhood conversation with her mother. It's interesting that Day's mother told her to stop talking about her "doughnut plan." All too often, we stop talking about our passion because it doesn't make sense or we don't see how we can possibly do it as an adult and yet make a living. To her credit, Day may have stopped talking about her plan, but she never stopped thinking about it. She took some social action to correct a problem in the best way she knew how.

My life purpose is to create order out of chaos. In my own life, I remember my favorite rainy-day activity was to disorganize my room so I could put it back in order! I remember "attacking" my father's messy garage as an eight-year-old in order to put it in order. When I did, I stood there and beheld my work with a strange sense of peace.

If your parents are still alive, maybe it's time to talk with them. If not, are there brothers, sisters, aunts, uncles, or close family friends you can talk to? Ask them what you were like and what they remember about you when you were a child. What did you talk about? What games did you play? Something may stand out to them that will provide you a clue as to your purpose.

I can't tell you when you will find your purpose. That varies from person to person. My objective is to help you identify it when it does come to you, so you won't dismiss it as insignificant or irrelevant information. Why not conduct an investigation into your past and see what purpose clues emerge? Write down everything you know already, plus any childhood clues you obtain from your family, and study your notes. Do you see any pattern? Don't panic if you don't, but keep adding to that page, so that one day you will look at it and realize you have all the pieces of the purpose puzzle, and the picture is clear.

WEEK #16
We Can't Do It Until We Know It

It seems that there's no end to the interest generated by the purpose message. Every week, I meet with many people individually and in groups to help them find their purpose. *The Monday Memo* regularly has purpose as its theme and focus, and I receive many inquiries and questions online throughout the week. I have found one recurring problem among those who aren't sure yet as to what their purpose is — trying to understand how they will fulfill it before they even know what it is.

I talk to wives who are concerned about how their purpose will affect their families, but when I ask them what their purpose is, they can't tell me. I talk to husbands who ask questions about finances, career changes, and time away from home. When I ask them what their purpose is, they often respond, "Well, it's sort of like, well, you know, to maybe encourage people and to, uh, glorify God. Yeah, that's it!" That's probably not it.

Until you have a clear statement of your purpose, everything after remains unclear. There's no way you can understand how your purpose will work itself out until you know what it is. Therefore, your primary job is not to figure out the outcome, but to have faith to find your purpose in the first place. When you do, the rest seems to fall in place, sometimes quickly, sometimes over a longer period of time.

It's absolutely critical that you make a clear sound when describing your purpose. The Apostle Paul wrote the following analogy in one of his letters:

Even in the case of lifeless things that make sounds, such as the flute or harp, how will anyone know what tune is being played unless there is a distinction in the notes? Again, if the trumpet does not sound a clear call, who will get ready for battle? (1 Corinthians 14:7-8).

Once you find your purpose and can clearly describe it in nonreligious terms, you will recognize the opportunities that come your way. Whether you're finding or fulfilling your purpose, there's one key element to your success, and that's faith. You can't "figure out" your purpose, nor can you then set out to accomplish it in the power of your own effort.

I've found it takes more faith to find your purpose than it does to fulfill it! That's why it's so critical you are clear on what it is. Once you see it, faith will rise in you to see it done. Your purpose is what Paul referred to as "the vision from heaven" (Acts 26:19). That can only come when heaven is ready to release it and you are ready to receive it.

It took a lot more time and effort to realize what my purpose was than to find its expression. Are you ready to find your purpose? I can't promise that you will find it this week, but I can urge you to have faith that you will find it, if not this week, then in the weeks to come. You will seek, work, and strive to define your purpose, but in all of that, you must trust that God will show it to you. When you see it, you will be like the parable found in Matthew 13:44:

> "The kingdom of heaven is like treasure hidden in a field. When a man found it, he hid it again, and then in his joy went and sold all he had and bought that field."

I hope God helps clarify your purpose. If it happens, you won't have problems knowing what to do. You'll go for it because you'll have found the treasure worth the pursuit.

WEEK #17

Why Are You Doing It?

I had a meeting with someone who had a job offer. It was a good job that she had done before and could undoubtedly do again with a high level of excellence and efficiency. There was only one problem: She didn't want to do it! There were others who hoped that she would want to do it. She valued their input and searched her heart to find some way to fulfill their expectations. She had to say "no" to their offer, however, and instead launched out on her own to find something better suited to her life purpose.

Defining yourself and setting a course that you feel good about are difficult things to do. It's often easier to follow the career path of least resistance, a path that often can provide job security. For years, I felt I was supposed to be a pastor. I tried to live up to those expectations that, to be honest, I put on myself. I thought that's what God wanted me to do. I was a pastor to please others, but I wasn't happy. Finally, I faced how unhappy I was and resigned. Since then, I've resisted attempts by friends and counselors to fashion me according to what they felt I should do. Instead, I set out on a path to define and fulfill my purpose.

Now you may be asking, "What about the will of God? Where does that come into play?" And those are good questions. My sense, however, is that God will give you the will and heart to do His work. There may be a season where you do something that crosses your will and separates you from your joy, but I don't think that can happen for very long.

There's a Bible verse from *The Living Bible* that reads: "For God is at work within you, helping you want to obey him, and then helping you do what he wants" (Philippians 2:13). God is working in you to give you a will and desire to fulfill His will and then helping you do what that will represents. Part of that help is His joy. A man named Nehemiah once said, "The joy of the Lord is your strength" (Nehemiah 8:10). If you have no joy in what you do, then you have no strength.

Why are you doing what you do? Why are you studying what you are studying? Why are you running the business that you are running? Is it to fulfill someone else's dreams and expectations? If so, is that a good enough reason to continue doing it? The answer may be "yes," but it also may be "no." That's something only you can answer. If you answer "no," then what are you prepared to do about it?

It may be time to be honest with yourself and face the fact that you can't live up to others' expectations. You must live your own life and fulfill your own purpose. If you do nothing else but face this reality, you will have taken a giant step to finding and fulfilling your purpose. May you find a breakthrough soon as you find the courage to define yourself. There's no one better suited for the job.

WEEK #18
Free To Be Me

I ran across another great quote as I was thinking about how hard it is to simply be yourself. Parents, family, educators, and friends may have told you that you can't do this or that because you won't be able to make a living, or because it just doesn't make sense to them. At other times, you may have been your own worst enemy, criticizing and putting down your own creativity and tendencies. I talk with many people who are spending more time and energy trying to be who they are not, instead of becoming the best expression of who God created them to be. I can't find who said this, so if you know, please pass the name on to me:

> *Work like you don't need the money.*
> *Love like you've never been hurt.*
> *Dance like nobody's watching.*
> *Sing like nobody's listening.*

Read that over a few times and let the words and message sink in. Those lines speak of freedom—freedom to be who God made you to be without concern for what others think. It also speaks of having freedom from past hurts, disappointments, and failures so that you can pursue the unique path that is yours. Finally, those lines set you free from yourself and your tendency to prematurely judge what you are becoming or doing.

There's a proverb that states, "The fear of man brings a snare" (Proverbs 29:25). If you can't be who you were created to be because you're afraid of what someone thinks, you have indeed fallen into a trap. Instead of responding to your inner voice, you are following outside voices that don't understand you or the path God has chosen for you. You need to give yourself permission to sing and dance like no one else is paying attention.

Why not spend some time discovering where you have limited your development because of what others think. Write down any areas or interests that you had a desire to pursue at one time only to have someone talk you out of them. Maybe you have talked yourself out of them. Whoever is to blame, determine to reestablish contact with the song and dance that are uniquely yours. As you do, I hope you'll take some steps, no matter how small, toward freedom of the mind and heart, freedom toward the fulfillment that comes from being true to the real you. I'm free to be me. I recommend it to you as a worthy goal.

WEEK #19
Permission To Be Creative

When I travel, I bring several books to read and study. On one trip, I brought *The Artist's Way* by Julia Cameron. The subtitle of this book is "A Spiritual Path to Higher Creativity," and it's a best seller, available in its tenth anniversary edition. The stated purpose of the book is to provide a course in discovering and recovering your creative self. I would recommend the book as a tool to develop the disciplines necessary for creativity.

There are many helpful tips throughout the book to help you unlock and release your creativity, such as:

- Stop telling yourself, "It's too late."
- Stop waiting until you make enough money to do something you'd really love.
- Stop telling yourself, "It's just my ego" whenever you yearn for a more creative life.
- Stop telling yourself that your dreams don't matter, that they are only dreams and that you should be more sensible.
- Stop fearing that your family and friends would think you crazy.
- Stop telling yourself that creativity is a luxury and that you should be grateful for what you've got.[8]

The author continues:

> As you learn to recognize, nurture, and protect your inner artist, you will be able to move beyond pain and creative constriction. You will learn ways to

recognize and resolve fear, remove emotional scar tissue, and strengthen your confidence. Damaging old ideas about creativity will be explored and discarded.

Do any of these statements apply to you? Maybe it's time you examined your own attitude toward creativity. Is your definition of creativity restricted to artists and writers? Maybe your creativity lies in other areas. Do you like to work with wood or metal? Are you a sculptor or someone who likes to work with ceramics? Or perhaps you are a seamstress, a cook, or a baker? Then again, you may have a house you've always wanted to design and build, or an idea for a business. Whatever your expression of creativity, what are you prepared to do about it? If nothing else, you may have to confront your low self-esteem concerning your creativity by going to the kitchen or workshop and getting your hands dirty.

This issue is critical if you are going to live a purposeful and productive life. You must learn to trust that which is within you, that which has come from God who is the source of all that is creative. I've gotten into the habit of studying creative people who were writers, actors, composers, or poets. I want to study those masters so I can become a master in my own right. Will you join me and explore and develop your creative side? I hope you will and that you'll give yourself permission to be creative.

WEEK #20

The Jonah Complex

The famous psychologist, Dr. Abraham Maslow, coined a term "The Jonah Complex." What did Maslow mean? We know that Jonah was an Old Testament prophet and that he had a short book that related part of his life story. Jonah was given an assignment by God to go and deliver a harsh message to a city and a people he didn't like. He didn't want to do it, so he got on a ship and went in the opposite direction from where he was told to go.

A storm arose during the trip, and it soon became clear to the sailors that Jonah was the cause of the storm. When they threw him overboard, the storm ceased and Jonah was swallowed by a whale; Jonah then spent three days and nights in the whale's stomach. After Jonah relented and agreed to go on God's mission, the whale spit him out and Jonah went on his way.

Maslow used "The Jonah Complex" to describe anyone who is running from their true life's calling. He went on to say, "If you deliberately set out to be less than you are capable of, you will never truly be happy."[9] This term accurately describes the condition of many people with whom I have come in contact. They are running from the greatness and creativity that is in them. They are afraid, not of failure, but of success.

So what do these people do who are trapped in "The Jonah Complex"? According to my experience, they spend a lot of time trying to weather the storm. They try to stay on the ship where they are, instead of jumping into the waves of life. They tell me they are "praying about it"—whatever the "it" is for them. Yet day after day, and sometimes year after year, goes by and they do nothing. Their prayer is actually a delay tactic, waiting for God to do something that only they can do.

What about you? Are you suffering from "The Jonah Complex"? Are you running from your purpose or from some significant thing that God has for you to do? Is your ship being tossed by the waves of financial lack, unhappiness, and lack of productivity, yet you stubbornly cling to the ship's mast, hoping that things will get better? I've found that many know their purpose but are afraid for whatever reason to walk it out. Perhaps it's time for you to face who you are and what God wants you to do. And perhaps it's time for you to take steps to get off your sinking ship and into the purpose of God. It may look more dangerous "out there," but the only danger lies in avoiding the great things that God has for you to do.

WEEK #21
Yes and No

I usually begin purpose seminars with Acts 6:1-4:

> In those days when the number of disciples was increasing, the Grecian Jews among them complained against the Hebraic Jews because their widows were being overlooked in the daily distribution of food. So the Twelve gathered all the disciples together and said, "It would not be right for us to neglect the ministry of the word of God in order to wait on tables. Brothers, choose seven men from among you who are known to be full of the Spirit and wisdom. We will turn this responsibility over to them and will give our attention to prayer and the ministry of the word."

I study this passage regularly, and it speaks to me every time I do. Three things impress me most:

- There were problems, even in the early church.
- The apostles could not solve or be involved in all the problems.
- The apostles focused on what they did best.

I like this passage so much because it portrays a problem you and I have all the time: when to say "yes" and when to say "no." The more successful you are, the more this problem seems to appear because success only leads to more opportunities and "open doors." I talk with people regularly who are facing those "open doors," but for whatever reason find themselves unable to walk through them.

Sometimes the problem is what you are currently

doing. It's familiar; you have had a measure of success or at least know more or less what's expected of you. The current situation may provide a safe environment in which to function. If you continue doing what you currently do, you won't be able to embrace that new thing, opportunity, or "open door" that's before you.

At other times, you may have an "open door," but as you begin to walk through, a new development in your current situation comes to confuse and distract you. It may be more money, a slight variation in your current routine, or an offer of some new responsibility that causes you to reconsider that "open door." The Apostle Paul wrote, "Because a great door for effective work has opened to me, and there are many who oppose me" (1 Corinthians 16:9). Sometimes the opposition presents itself as a chance to stay in your comfort zone where you know the people and the routine.

I ran across a quote this week that may help. It is from Baruch Spinoza, a 17th century Dutch philosopher. He wrote, "A good thing which prevents us from enjoying a greater good is in truth an evil." I'm sure the apostles in Acts 6 saw helping the widows as a good thing, but helping them would have taken them away from something better. Thus, they declined to get personally involved.

Ask yourself if some good thing is keeping you from a better thing and has thus become a bad thing for you. If the answer is "yes," then what are you prepared to do about it? Do you have the courage and faith to face that good thing and stop doing it? Are you prepared to say "no" to find your greater "yes"? Don't settle for good when you can have the best. You owe it to God, yourself, and others not to do that.

WEEK #22

A Letter From Jacquie

I received an email one time that perfectly portrayed what I want for your life. Let me share it with you:

Dear Mr. Stanko,

I felt a need to write and thank you for the beautiful *Monday Memos*. They have altered the course of my life and I just want to share the wonderful miracles that have happened to me.

I was feeling that my life had no purpose and I was lost. I came across *The Monday Memo* and things began to change. I found direction and my purpose was made clear to me in my prayers. For years I have wanted to go to America to learn how to help autistic children. You see, I have an autistic son, but such a trip has never worked out. After 5 years I thought I would try again. Well, to cut a long story short, I am going to finally make the trip and learn how to help my son! When I get back to Zimbabwe, I am going to start a school here that will help other autistic and mentally-challenged children. Since I have found my purpose and my dream, I feel alive. I am bubbling inside and feel like I am bouncing off the ceiling and walls.

It is a miracle. I am a single parent with three children and not finding it easy living in this environment where everything goes up on a daily basis. The thought of a trip to America seemed impossible. I had faith and believed that if it was meant to be, it would happen. I was given the money for my ticket, and I was also given a huge scholarship for the education and accommodation in America. I also received a visa, which is another impossible task in this country. God has smoothed my road and is helping me to achieve my dream. I am just so very happy and grateful. I leave soon and feel so very, very blessed.

I want to thank you from the bottom of my heart for helping me on my way by making me think differently. God bless you and the wonderful work that you do.

—Jacquie

No, Jacquie, I must thank you. Thank you for having the faith to pursue both your purpose and the means to achieve it. Thank you too for turning a difficult situation into one that will bless not only your family but so many others. On behalf of purpose seekers everywhere, thank you for giving us a powerful example of faith and purpose.

When I read Jacquie's letter, I thought of an anonymous poem that I found years ago:

There's no thrill in easy sailing
*   when the skies are clear and blue.*
There's no joy in merely doing things
*   that anyone can do.*
But there is some satisfaction
*   that is mighty sweet to take.*
When you reach a destination
*   that you thought you'd never make.*

Wherever you are in your purpose journey, I hope that you are closer to your destination. If you are discouraged with the journey, don't give up. You may be closer than you think to writing someone a letter like Jacquie wrote me. Happy trails!

WEEK #23
What Do You Fear?

I purchased a new laptop computer a couple years ago. I put off getting it, even though many of the keys and features on my old one didn't function any longer. Why did I hesitate? It wasn't only because of the cost; it was also because I was afraid of the change from the old one to the new.

What was I afraid of? I was afraid my technical ignorance would show. I was also afraid of losing data in the transfer, or of being on the road somewhere and the new unit would fail to operate. I was even afraid of choosing the wrong unit to replace the old one. Those fears kept me from making a decision. After I made the purchase, I was relieved, although I spent more than a few hours working to get the new computer just the way I desired it to be.

You may want to ask yourself, "What am I afraid of?" In my discussions with many people, I have found three basic fears that can keep people from being purposeful and productive. They are:

- Fear of others
- Fear of failure
- Fear of looking foolish

Let's address the first one on the list. A wise writer once wrote: "Fear of man will prove to be a snare, but whoever trusts in the Lord is kept safe" (Proverbs 29:25).

I get many emails from people who are afraid of their supervisor, pastor, spouse or counselor. This fear keeps them bound to the past so they can't respond in faith to the future. They can't embrace change, not because they fear the change but because they fear people's reaction to their change.

The second fear is of failure. I know how painful failures can be because I've had my share of them. But failures have been great teachers, and every failure has produced enough wisdom to prepare me for future success. I'm reminded of that well-known Bible verse that states: "And we know that in all things God works for the good of those who love him, who have been called according to his purpose" (Romans 8:28).

God is working in all things for you. Don't go looking for failure and don't do stupid things expecting God to cover you. If you are facing a decision that lines up with your purpose and God's will for your life, then take the next step toward achieving that purpose, without fear of failure. If you should fail, learn from it and move on.

Finally, if you're afraid of looking foolish, then perhaps you had better go live in a desert where no one can see you. Learning and growing can make you look awkward. Think of it like a child learning to walk. They look foolish as they take a few steps and fall, yet they persevere with the encouragement of their family. They overcome their foolishness only to enter into the next learning experience that has the potential to make them look just as foolish. Jesus said:

> "Do not be afraid, little flock, for your Father has been pleased to give you the kingdom. Sell your possessions and give to the poor. Provide purses for yourselves that will not wear out, a treasure in heaven that will not be exhausted, where no thief comes near and no moth destroys. For where your treasure is, there your heart will be also" (Luke 12:32-34).

Determine not to yield to fear any longer! It wasn't until I began to face my fears that I was able to overcome them. Today I still deal with fear, but I no longer let it be my master. I now ask myself, "John, what are you afraid of?" and then I proceed. I would urge you to do the same.

WEEK #24

What You Do Isn't Who You Are

I read and enjoyed a book by Os Guinness, entitled *Entrepreneurs of Life: Faith and the Venture of Purposeful Living*. As I read, I began to reflect on the difference between one's occupation and one's purpose. As the word implies, an occupation is what uses up our time and energy. Your occupation is what pays the bills, but it isn't necessarily what defines who you are. To further explain, let's look at the Apostle Paul's life.

Paul's purpose was to bring the gospel of Christ to the Gentile world. We know that because his "call" on the Damascus road has a prominent place in the book of Acts. In every epistle that Paul wrote, he made some reference to his purpose, usually relating his purpose to some Old Testament passage. When Paul talked about himself, he referred to his purpose, yet that purpose wasn't his occupation.

To earn a living, Paul made tents. When he moved into an area and lacked funds, he went to work as a tent maker. Yet Paul never talked or wrote about his occupation. The only way we know that Paul made tents was that Luke wrote about it in the book of Acts. Don't you find it interesting that Paul never referred to it? That was what he did, but it wasn't who he was. He was an apostle to the Gentiles and that is what got the choice place in his heart, time, efforts, and writings.

Who are you? I'm not asking what you do. You may sell insurance, but who are you? You may also be a missionary to some people group, while selling insurance pays the bills. When people ask you what you do, like I just did, how do you respond? Do you say that you're an insurance salesperson or a missionary? If you answer that you're a salesperson, then you're defining yourself according to what you do. If you say missionary, you're focusing on purpose and not on what provides your food and pays the bills. You may only get to the mission field once a year on your vacation time, but the other weeks you're praying and working toward that mission. You don't have to quit your occupation to embrace your purpose. You may simply need to distinguish between the two.

Guinness wrote, in the book I mentioned above, the following paragraph (since he uses the words "calling" and "vocation" for purpose, I have taken the liberty of inserting the word "purpose" where appropriate):

> Calling [purpose] helps us finish [our lives] well because it prevents us from confusing the termination of our occupations with the termination of our vocations [purpose]. If we ever limit our calling [purpose] to what we do, and that task is taken away from us—we suddenly find ourselves unemployed, retired, or pronounced terminally ill—then we are tempted to depression and doubt. What has happened? We have let our occupation become so intertwined with our vocation [purpose] that losing the occupation means losing the sense of vocation [purpose] too.[10]

Have you either not found or lost your sense of purpose? Perhaps you have confused the difference between what you do and who you are. I would suggest you take time to reflect on this important distinction. No longer be content to define your life in terms of what you do but rather who you are. It will make all the difference in the world.

WEEK #25
Dealing With Discouragement

If you are discouraged while trying to find your purpose, I understand how you feel. It can be hard work! I can guarantee that you'll find your purpose, but I can't tell you when that will happen! The search can be long and frustrating. I heard a principle shared once by someone who was looking for their place in God's plan. This person began to thank God for his purpose before he knew what it was. Now that's faith!

Thanking God for what you already have before you see or know it is consistent with faith, for Paul wrote: "As it is written: 'I have made you [Abraham] a father of many nations.' He is our father in the sight of God, in whom he believed—the God who gives life to the dead and calls things that are not as though they were" (Romans 4:17). God seems to talk about things that are not as though they are. Why don't you do the same? Talk about and thank God for your purpose as if you already know it. It's just a matter of time before you do.

If you know your purpose, but are discouraged in fulfilling it, why not try something new? I want you to close your eyes and picture yourself doing what you were created to do. See yourself conducting an orchestra, singing a song, working with wood, or running your business. When I'm writing a book and I get discouraged with its progress, I close my eyes and picture myself signing that book and handing it to someone. Before I have it finished, I choose to "see" it finished and being given to someone else (who is always smiling when they receive it). For some strange reason, that image always encourages me to keep writing. When I do this, I feel like I'm borrowing some joy from tomorrow to take pleasure in today.

Finally, if you know your purpose but for some reason find yourself in a down time, do what I did recently. The phone wasn't ringing, I had some cancellations, and money was a bit scarce. So I began to read the emails and letters I received over the last year. I chose to focus on what God has already done, believing that He would open doors for me to do it again.

When there's no one around to encourage you, then you sometimes have to encourage yourself. Remember the lives you've touched, the songs you've written, or the other success stories of which you've been part. If you don't already, begin to save up mementos of your successes so you can refer to them in your down times.

Finally, sometimes you need a friend who can perk you up when you're down. Don't be too proud or afraid to call them. Sometimes other people can see your purpose and productivity more clearly than you. Still others can point out your potential while you are still in the development stage. Listen to what they have to say! And if I can be of assistance, please don't hesitate to write me. I'm familiar with many of the pitfalls on the road of purpose and will be glad to encourage you along the way as you battle your discouragement.

WEEK #26

For God, In God

Once while teaching in Zimbabwe, I talked about the difference between doing things *in God* and doing things *for God*. When you are working in God, you are working with the strength and energy that God provides. When you are working for God, you usually work in your own strength and the results are seldom what you want. When Moses was working for God, he killed an Egyptian. Later, when he worked in God, he raised his staff and the entire Egyptian army was destroyed. That's the difference between "in-God" and "for-God" results. When you find and work in your life purpose, you almost always produce "in-God" results; that's why knowing your purpose is so important.

I was recently reading about John Wesley, the founder of the Methodist church. John Wesley found his purpose and therefore was able to produce "in-God" results. Read on and see what I mean: Wesley would preach three times a day, beginning at 5:00 a.m. since workers could stop to hear him as they walked to their daily drudgery. He sometimes covered 60 miles a day on horseback. Weather conditions made no difference; he made his schedule and kept it regardless. He would flee an angry mob by jumping into a cold pond, swim out, and go on to preach again. He had the ability to turn hostile people his way. In all he went to Ireland 42 times and to Scotland 22 times.

John Wesley taught as much by example as by his measured sermons. He published many volumes for use in devotions and turned profits into such projects as a dispensary for the poor. His personal life was beyond reproach. He translated hymns, interpreted scripture, wrote hundreds of letters, trained hundreds of men and women, and kept in his journals a record of expended energy that has hardly a rival in western literature.

He made this diary entry on Tuesday, June 28, 1774:

> This being my birthday, the first day of my seventy-second year, I was considering: How is this, that I find just the same strength as I did thirty years ago? That my sight is considerably better now, and my nerves firmer than they were then? That I have none of the infirmities of old age, and have lost several I had in my youth? The grand reason is the good pleasure of God, who doth whatsoever pleaseth him. The chief means are: 1) my constantly rising at four, for about fifty years; 2) my generally preaching at five in the morning, one of the most healthy exercises in the world; 3) my never travelling less, by sea or land, than four thousand five hundred miles a year.

During his ministry, Wesley rode over 250,000 miles on horseback, a distance equal to ten circuits of the globe along the equator. He preached over 40,000 sermons. Today his followers number 40 million people.[11]

Ask yourself whether or not you are achieving "in-God" or "for-God" results. Are you accomplishing all that you were created to do, or are you achieving far below your potential? If you aren't happy with your results, then maybe you need to meditate on the difference between working in God or for God. I trust that you will find a way to work in God and that you will change the world, just as John Wesley did.

WEEK #27

What Makes You Cry?

There's a man in the Bible named Nehemiah who was the cupbearer for the king. In other words, he was a butler or a servant. We aren't told how he came to this trusted position, and we don't know much about Nehemiah's background. He just shows up on the scene as a servant. Service to others is how many of God's leaders were prepared for leadership: If you are a servant leader, someone may take your leadership away, but they can never take away your ability or desire to serve. That's the constant factor in every servant leader's life.

That isn't what I want to show you from the life of Nehemiah. While he was serving, a group of people came to visit from Jerusalem:

> The words of Nehemiah son of Hacaliah: In the month of Kislev in the twentieth year, while I was in the citadel of Susa, Hanani, one of my brothers, came from Judah with some other men, and I questioned them about the Jewish remnant that survived the exile, and also about Jerusalem. They said to me, "Those who survived the exile and are back in the province are in great trouble and disgrace. The wall of Jerusalem is broken down, and its gates have been burned with fire" (Nehemiah 1:1-3).

First of all, Nehemiah questioned the men from Jerusalem. He was interested in Jerusalem, so he asked questions. What are *you* interested in? What causes you ask to questions? What is your burden? What do you like to read and study?

The first indication Nehemiah was pursuing his life

purpose, without even knowing it, was that he was simply asking probing questions about a special interest he had. The real indicator of his purpose is found in the next verse:

> When I heard these things, I sat down and wept. For some days I mourned and fasted and prayed before the God of heaven (Nehemiah 1:4).

When Nehemiah heard the report about the poor conditions in Jerusalem, he cried. What makes you angry, what moves you to fast and call out to the God of heaven, and what makes you weep are often indications of your purpose. I'm sure others heard the same report about Jerusalem that Nehemiah heard, but none of the others were moved as he was. You see, his purpose was to rebuild the city of his fathers, which he did by first rebuilding the walls and then repopulating the city.

You may not know your purpose yet because the situation that will release and define your purpose isn't ready to receive you. Maybe you will rebuild something that isn't yet in need of repair. Or perhaps you will invent something but the technology for your invention isn't quite in place yet. Maybe you will save something or someone who isn't even lost at this time.

That doesn't mean you can't be preparing. Nehemiah was serving the king. You don't serve the king unless you're good at what you do. It's safe to assume Nehemiah was committed to excellence and producing superior work. When you don't know your purpose, pursuing excellence is always a good way to prepare.

I encourage you to spend some time trying to answer the questions I've raised in this study. Identify what makes you cry or become angry. Reassess your commitment to excellence and make sure it's where it needs to be. Be willing to pay any price to find and fulfill your purpose, even if you're still searching for what it is. If you'll do that, then a situation will present itself to you just as it did to Nehemiah. At that point, all that you've been through will suddenly make sense.

Week #28

Children, Parents, and Purpose

I had the privilege of attending a Billy Graham Crusade in Dallas one time. There's no greater example of someone fulfilling his life purpose than Billy Graham. Dr. Graham conducted crusades for over 50 years and changed the world by doing what he did best, over and over again.

I wonder whether Billy Graham's parents saw their son's life purpose? I ask because I have been thinking about Moses and his parents. "At that time Moses was born, and he was no ordinary child. For three months he was cared for in his father's house" (Acts 7:20). What did Moses' parents see that enabled them to recognize their son was not ordinary?

When our son was born, his nose was flat against his face. His hair was standing straight up, even though it was wet. Not only that, but his ears stood out and he was various shades of red, purple, and pink all over his little body. When the nurse handed him to his mother, she looked and him and said, "Maybe he'll be intelligent!" (I'm glad to report that he has grown to be an intelligent *and* handsome adult!)

I think Moses' parents looked at him and saw his purpose. At the time of Moses' birth, Pharaoh ordered all male babies to be thrown into the river. Moses' parents didn't throw him in, however, at least not right away. They cared for and hid him for three months; then complied with Pharaoh's orders. When they did, they put him in a basket first. You know the rest: Pharaoh's daughter found Moses and raised him as her own.

Because his parents saw his purpose, Moses was able to know it as well, probably at an early age. We read:

He saw one of them being mistreated by an Egyptian, so he went to his defense and avenged him by killing the Egyptian. Moses thought that his own people would realize that God was using him to rescue them, but they did not (Acts 7:24-25).

Moses knew he was to rescue Israel, but there were two problems: Israel didn't recognize his purpose and Moses tried to fulfill it in his own strength by killing Egyptians. What a long road he had to go, killing one Egyptian at a time. He probably said to himself, "One down, three million to go!" Later, after 40 years in the wilderness, Moses rescued Israel, not with a sword, but with his shepherd's staff.

Just as Moses' parents saw his purpose, parents today still have the ability and responsibility to do the same for their children. Our daughter obtained a wonderful job with a great company because she is a gifted salesperson. We saw that gift when she was only four years old. We tried to keep it before her as she went through university and now she is operating in her purpose. A parent plays a big part in directing children in the way they ought to go as determined by their purpose. What do you see in your children? What makes them extraordinary in the sight of God and men?

When we can't see purpose for ourselves, often there are others that clearly see our purpose, just as we can do for our children. We need to seek the advice and input of trusted advisers and use them as a guide to find our way home to our life purpose.

And finally, there's no minimum age to know your purpose. Moses, Samuel, David, and Joseph, just to name a few, all knew their life purpose when they were young. A young person can know their purpose, and no one should discount what they're seeing, no matter how young the person seeing it may be.

I trust that you will apply this insight to your life and the lives of your children, friends, and associates. Look to see what makes these people extraordinary and maybe one of them will take their place on the world's stage, just as Billy Graham did. There are no age restrictions when it comes to purpose.

WEEK #29

Knowing the Will of God

I'm impressed with how many people write me, concerned about "missing the Lord." They want to do God's will and find their purpose, but they don't want to do or say the wrong thing.

Consequently, some are so concerned about "missing the Lord" that they may actually be "missing the Lord." If your fear of doing the wrong thing leads you to do nothing, then your faith does not have a way to express itself. James wrote, "In the same way, faith by itself, if it is not accompanied by action, is dead" (James 2:17). And without faith, it is impossible to please God (see Hebrews 11:6).

You need to have confidence in the God to whom you pray. Your ability to be heard and receive an answer does not depend on your prayer but on the faithfulness of the God to whom you pray. There's no correct or incorrect formula when you talk to God. You talk and He listens. And then He answers. Let's look at two important passages that highlight this point. The first is found in Luke 11:9-13:

> So I say to you: "Ask and it will be given to you; seek and you will find; knock and the door will be opened to you. For everyone who asks receives; he who seeks finds; and to him who knocks, the door will be opened. Which of you fathers, if your son asks for a fish, will give him a snake instead? Or if he asks for an egg, will give him a scorpion? If you then, though you are evil, know how to give good gifts to your children, how much more will your Father in heaven give the Holy Spirit to those who ask him!"

If you ask the Father to help you find your purpose, He will hear you. He isn't going to trick you or send you a misleading message. He's your Father, and He will give you what you ask. If you ask God to know and do His will and then think about writing a book, that probably isn't your idea. It's God answering your prayer!

The second verse is in John 7:17. The Pharisees were asking whether Jesus was sent from the Father or not. And Jesus replied by saying, "If any man is willing to do His will, he shall know of the teaching, whether it is of God, or [whether] I speak from Myself" (NAS). Often, the key to finding the will of God for your life is to make a commitment to do it before you know what it is. In essence, Jesus said to the Pharisees, "If you set your will to do God's will, you will always know what His will is!" You may say that it isn't that simple, but I maintain that it is.

How does this apply to purpose and productivity? If you have prayed, God has heard you. You don't have to worry about "missing His will." You just have to act in faith on what you think you have received. St. Augustine once said, "I pray and then I do what I want." St. Augustine wasn't advocating self will; he was just confident that the God to whom He prayed was able to shape his will in response to prayer.

I want you to ask God for something you don't know or understand. Maybe you need to find your purpose or want to set a godly goal you can work toward. Before you have the answer, I want you to commit to do or say whatever He shows you before you actually know what it is! Then I want you to have faith your Father isn't going to trick you and give you a stone instead of the bread for which you are asking. Don't be concerned about "missing God," but be ready to find and do His will. I am confident the God to whom you pray will help you as you seek purposeful direction.

WEEK #30

Toxic Relationships

I enjoy studying the lives of two men in the Old Testament—David and Jonathan. David and Jonathan were more than friends; they were covenant brothers. They had a special relationship and recognized this relationship by making a special covenant as you see in 1 Samuel 18. Later, when David was avoiding Jonathan's father, King Saul, Jonathan uttered these remarkable words:

> "Don't be afraid," he said. "My father Saul will not lay a hand on you. You will be king over Israel, and I will be second to you. Even my father Saul knows this." The two of them made a covenant before the Lord. Then Jonathan went home, but David remained at Horesh (1 Samuel 23:17-18).

Why are these words so remarkable? Jonathan was the king's son, the heir apparent and the second in command. Here, he acknowledged that David's purpose was to be king and his purpose was to serve David as his right-hand man. Jonathan relinquished his claim to the throne and expressed his willingness to accept the purpose God had for him.

Even though Jonathan knew this and spoke about it, however, it never came to pass. Jonathan died in battle with his father: "The Philistines pressed hard after Saul and his sons, and they killed his sons Jonathan, Abinadab and Malki-Shua" (1 Samuel 31:2). I have a question to ask you. With the knowledge Jonathan had, what was he doing with his worthless father, going into a battle that could not be won? Because Jonathan could not deal with his father, he forfeited his right to fulfill his purpose. He died and David mourned him for the rest of his life. Saul had become a toxic relationship where Jonathan's purpose was concerned.

What does this have to do with you and me? It's important that we follow God's will for our lives and not let relationships hinder us. We can't allow our supervisor, pastor, friends or family hinder us from pursuing and fulfilling our purpose. No matter how tough the situation, we must steward our purpose. We must oversee it and not allow anyone to talk us out of it or keep us from being the fullest, best expression of who God created us to be.

You need to take an honest look at your life and purpose. Have you listened to a negative, discouraging, toxic report from someone about you and your abilities? Have you put your purpose on the shelf to please or serve someone else? Have you spent time trying to tell God why you aren't the one to do what it is that is in your heart? As you answer these questions, please remember Jonathan. Jonathan knew his purpose but lost it because he could not admit that his father was a toxic scoundrel who did not have anyone's best interests at heart but his own. You'll answer to no one but God for the results of what He has assigned you to do. I urge you to determine in your heart to make pleasing Him your top priority, even at the risk of disappointing someone you love.

WEEK #31

Nancy's Story

Several months ago, I was teaching a seminar and thought about my friend Nancy. I wanted to share with them the impact one of my first purpose seminars had on her and felt I needed to make sure I had her story correct. Through a mutual friend, I contacted Nancy and asked her to write about what has happened in her life the last 12 years. Here's her reply:

> I remember hearing you teach on purpose in your *Life is a GoldMine: Can You Dig It* seminar. At that time, I was at a critical point in my faith journey. I ached for more creative expression in my life. Being the daughter of the sports editor for our local paper, writing came naturally and easy for me. I loved words and I had always loved music. Little did I realize that your seminar would be one of the things God would use to help me find the courage to believe and pursue the desires of my heart, namely songwriting. First, I had to acknowledge the desire that I wanted to write to myself, to God, and to family and friends. Then I began to actively pursue this dream and desire one day at a time, one step at a time. I remember the phrase "never despise small beginnings." Maybe I heard it from you.
>
> Now, some years later, I have published more than 300 songs, written 12 musicals (children and adult), have had four songs nominated for a Dove Award, and created the children's praise character Miss PattyCake. The Miss PattyCake line how

has 6 videos and 2 CD's, which I helped to write and create. I just finished my first book, to be published and released in March, which will be *A Miss PattyCake Easter Story*.

As a speaker, writer, worship leader, and a creative consultant, I desire to increase my speaking venues and to write several books. I now have my own publishing company, Mother's Heart Music and Mother's Heart Ministries. They both exist to nurture, inspire, and encourage all people to experience and know the love of God.

You would have to know Nancy to fully appreciate this report. She is neither wealthy, nor is she "well connected" in the music industry. (I write this because often we put successful people in a special category and lose the encouragement they can be for us.) She is a "regular person" like you and me who decided one day to step out "to actively pursue this dream and desire, one day at a time, one step at a time." She gave God something to bless and He did. And the exciting thing is that she isn't finished. God has more for her to do and she is still young (well, she's around my age, which is looking younger all the time!).

Like Nancy, your journey can begin right now. And your journey will start where hers did when you acknowledge to yourself, to God, and to others what it is that you want and were created to do. They may laugh, yawn or misunderstand. Their reaction (or lack of it) isn't important because you're not saying it for them. You're saying it for you and for God who put that dream in you in the first place. And you're saying it to release the dynamic of a spoken vision as outlined in these passages:

> Surely then you will find delight in the Almighty and will lift up your face to God. You will pray to him, and he will hear you, and you will fulfill your vows. What you decide on will be done, and light

will shine on your ways. When men are brought low and you say, "Lift them up!" then he will save the downcast. He will deliver even one who is not innocent, who will be delivered through the cleanness of your hands (Job 22:26-30).

If you don't have anyone else to tell, then write and tell me. Just tell someone, and then, remembering Nancy's story, get started creating your own.

WEEK #32

Opposition

I was reflecting on the Christmas story and how much turmoil Jesus' birth caused. Consider Mary, who became pregnant outside of marriage, or so Joseph and her family thought. We see Joseph, who was ready to divorce Mary until the angel appeared and told him to do otherwise. We see Mary making a trip on foot and by donkey to Bethlehem while she was nine months pregnant. When she arrived, she had to give birth in an outdoor stable. Later, King Herod, who heard about Jesus and perceived that He was a threat to his throne, had all the male children two years or younger killed in Bethlehem. Yes, the birth of Jesus wasn't exactly the best of times for those closely involved.

That's how tough things can get when you function in your purpose. Until you clarify your purpose, life can be peaceful, perhaps uneventful. Once you set out on a course to fulfill your purpose, however, all heaven and some of hell can break loose. You may even find that you have enemies simply because you are trying to do what you were created to do.

In the book of Genesis, Joseph wasn't popular with his brothers, but after he had his dreams that his purpose would be to rule over them, they conspired to kill him. Moses was successful in Egypt until he began to rescue his people. Then Egypt and Pharaoh became his enemies. David was a shepherd boy who became a popular and successful servant of King Saul. After David was anointed to be king (his purpose), Saul persecuted him. In the New Testament, a man named Saul was a successful Jewish evangelist and theologian until his fateful trip on the Damascus road. After that, Jews, and even some of his fellow believers, became a source of suffering and pain.

Then there was Jesus. He stirred up some enemies at birth and then seemed to settle into a simple lifestyle in Nazareth for the next 30 years. When He began to fulfill His purpose to seek and save the lost, He found many ready to oppose and even kill Him. Are you seeing a pattern here? Your purpose can produce circumstances that are painful and even dangerous. If you understand this, you'll see that the opposition is actually a confirmation that you're doing something right, not something wrong. Your purpose is so powerful that it will usually threaten someone, maybe even someone close to you, someone from whom you would not expect such opposition.

I urge you to spend a few minutes reflecting on the price that Jesus paid for you to enjoy what you have. Then I hope you will resolve to be a man or woman of purpose, to be a person who will see your enemies and opponents for what they are: a confirmation of the correct path you are pursuing. If you're encountering opposition, have hope! If you're afraid to embrace your purpose because it may make someone unhappy, take courage! If Joseph, Moses, David, Paul, and Jesus had enemies, you will too. They made their purpose their life, and the rest is history. I trust you will join them and make some history of your own.

WEEK #33
Enjoy Your Work

Let's look at a familiar passage in Ecclesiastes 3:1-13:

> There is a time for everything, and a season for every activity under heaven: a time to be born and a time to die, a time to plant and a time to uproot, a time to kill and a time to heal, a time to tear down and a time to build, a time to weep and a time to laugh, a time to mourn and a time to dance, a time to scatter stones and a time to gather them, a time to embrace and a time to refrain, a time to search and a time to give up, a time to keep and a time to throw away, a time to tear and a time to mend, a time to be silent and a time to speak, a time to love and a time to hate, a time for war and a time for peace. What does the worker gain from his toil? I have seen the burden God has laid on men. He has made everything beautiful in its time. He has also set eternity in the hearts of men; yet they cannot fathom what God has done from beginning to end. I know that there is nothing better for men than to be happy and do good while they live. That everyone may eat and drink, and find satisfaction in all his toil—this is the gift of God.

Do you have satisfaction in your work? If not, then perhaps the reason for your dissatisfaction can be found in verse two, which states that there is a time to be born and a time to die. The key to your satisfaction may be in not trying to keep something alive but in seeing something die, even something that has become special to you.

It's hard to discern the seasons of life and work in which you find yourself. Something that began with such hope and energy may now be something that is taking from you the very life that it once gave. I regularly receive emails from people who were trying to fit 28 hours of work into a 24-hour day. There's just no way to do that. I encourage each person who writes to find what it is they need to stop doing and then focus on what needs to be done.

Activities, roles, and even businesses, ministries, and churches have a time to be born and then have a time to die. That's a part of the life cycle. Trying to keep something alive that is past its season of life is not only counterproductive, but also impossible. If you are like many people, you may regularly set goals and resolutions. If those resolutions have any chance of being fulfilled, something else may have to come to an end before it can begin.

This isn't easy to do. It's not easy to end something that still has life and that you still enjoy doing. If you want to be purposeful and productive, you must regularly determine what stage or season your activities are in. Should they continue or should they end so new activities or direction can emerge in the coming days? All I can say as I face this process is "His will be done." I pray the same for you.

WEEK #34

Flavored Water

Jesus said: "Whoever believes in me, as the Scripture has said, streams of living water will flow from within him. By this he meant the Spirit, whom those who believed in him were later to receive" (John 7:38-39). If you have faith in Jesus, He promised something would come from you like a river or streams of living water that has life for you and others. In other words, Jesus promised you would be in a flow of life that would sustain you and others around you.

The waters that flow from you, while coming from the Spirit's presence, will have *your* flavor. Those waters should "taste" like you; they should have the taste of your experience, gifts, and purpose. Many people, in trying to be spiritual, distance themselves from who they are and try to be someone they are not. God made you as you are and comes into your life not to radically change you but to make the fullest, best expression of who He intended for you to be in the first place.

When you sing, the Spirit may be flowing from you, but it's *your* voice. When you counsel, the Spirit may be using you to help someone, but you're doing it utilizing *your* style and counseling technique. Even the writers of the gospels, who were writing the inspired word of God, used words, phrases, and grammatical styles unique to them. The water that flowed out of them tasted like them, but it has brought the Spirit's life to many throughout the ages.

The water that comes from you and me must not be artificially flavored. We don't have to be like someone else to fulfill our purpose or to please God. We are free to be us, to find a flow of life and purpose that comes naturally and touches others. We don't have to try and eliminate any and all flavor from our water. God is working in and through us for His good pleasure.

If you love music, then love it with all your heart and allow God to use that love to flavor your water. If you're a businessperson, then let the flavor of commerce or sales be what people taste when they "drink" from you.

Now there are some tastes that you must work to keep out of your flowing streams. First, there must not be any salt in your water (see James 3:12) that comes from cursing or gossiping. And there must not be any bitter taste in your water from grumbling or complaining about your circumstances (see Exodus 15:23). And, of course, there must not be any poison in your water that comes from sin or unresolved issues of the past (see Numbers 5:22-27). Apart from these things that can taint your water, you and I are to let the rivers flow, rivers of purpose that God will use to water our families, our nations, and even the world.

Sometimes we can be ambivalent about our flavor. We can feel that we aren't dynamic or exciting enough to be productive. You can be biased toward your own creativity and personality. When that happens, you'll work to restrict your flow because you don't think you have anything worth giving out to the world. I know that part of what I do is to help people remove the restrictions to their flow. Many people have told me, "Your message is so liberating! I feel free to be who I have been all along."

Is there water flowing from you, and does it taste like you? Have you "dammed up" the flow due to fear, confusion, or doubt? What flavor are you? Are your waters vintage you, or have they been injected by the taste of someone else or of elements that make the water undrinkable? I hope you will determine to have faith and let your rivers flow. Be yourself and let your purpose flavor the water of life that comes from you. If you taste good to God, why would you want to change?

WEEK #35
Courage

When I talk with people, trying to help them clarify their purpose, I usually ask them one question: What are you afraid of? It's the question I would ask you in this essay. Don't be too quick to answer as we examine this question together. In fact, you may want to take a minute and list four of five things that come to mind as you try to face your fears.

When I first decided to develop the *Seven Steps of a PurposeQuest* seminar, I was excited and anxious. In the three months it took to develop, I believe I faced just about every fear possible. What if no one comes? What if the weather is bad? What if the material isn't relevant? What if no one comes? What if I lose money? What if no one comes? (You can tell that my greatest fear was that no one would come!)

Someone once told me that courage isn't action in the absence of fear; it's action in the presence of fear. As I've studied fear, I came across an interesting Bible verse:

> But the cowardly [fearful], the unbelieving, the vile, the murderers, the sexually immoral, those who practice magic arts, the idolaters and all liars-their place will be in the fiery lake of burning sulfur. This is the second death (Revelation 21:8).

I can see why most of those listed end up in the fiery lake, but I was surprised to find the cowardly there. It seems that inaction due to unbelief or fear of failure is more serious in God's sight than I had previously considered it to be.

I've played enough sports to know that you can't perform while you're afraid. You just have to play and let your instincts take over. If you have to think about what you're doing, then usually you won't be effective on the field. You practice to hone your skills, but then you let it all flow in the game. There are many people who can't "flow" because they're afraid. Are you one of those people?

Now back to the question at hand: What are you afraid of? Fear can paralyze you and cause you to put off what you should be doing. In other words, fear can cause you to be disobedient. Face your fears and then take some step to do something you've wanted but have been afraid to do. Don't wait for your fear to go away, but in the midst of it, in spite of it, I want you to write the letter, make the phone call, talk to your supervisor or pastor, or make plans to do something bold. Make these coming days ones of courage and act on your dreams and purpose. As you do, you will join the army of God where only the courageous action in faith will bring victory.

WEEK #36

Small Is Good

One of my purpose heroes is George Washington Carver, the famous African-American scientist who lived in the period following the American Civil War. At a time when Americans of color suffered unspeakable conditions and prejudice, Carver single-handedly revolutionized agriculture in the American South, and he did it through work and prayer.

From his platform at Tuskegee Institute in Alabama, Carver urged farmers to plant peanuts, having discovered that peanuts were a perfect crop for the southern soil and climate. There was only one problem: at that time there was no market for peanuts! Farmers were angry and Carver was embarrassed. George Washington Carver prayed, and God gave him the solution to his problem.

The story has it that Carver began his prayer by asking, "Oh Lord, teach me about the universe," to which the Lord responded, "That is too much for you." Then Carver prayed, "Then Lord, teach me about man." Again the Lord responded, "You are still thinking too big." Finally, Carver cried out, "Lord, then please teach me about the peanut!" From that prayer, Carver went back to his simple laboratory and discovered more than 300 uses for the peanut over the course of his illustrious career. He found ways to make fertilizer, paint, and glue from peanuts and discovered peanut oil and peanut butter. While he was at it, he also discovered more than 100 uses for sweet potatoes.

The lessons from Carver's life for you and me are basic. First of all, prayer works. If you need wisdom or insight, why not ask God for it? Second, you need to keep things small.

You don't need to think about changing the world to serve God; you just need to think about how to change *your* world. Armed with the knowledge of your purpose and prayer, you can discover a significant breakthrough that will touch a few or many. You may be able to take what seems like a simple interest and turn it into a historic career, just like George Washington Carver did. Third, there are many discoveries yet to be made. Why can't you and I be the ones who discover them?

Ask God for wisdom concerning the interests you have, no matter how small or simple they may seem to be. And then expect God to answer you. Be ready to learn new things about the seemingly small interests in your life and then yield them to God. From that, there's no telling what God can do with you and through you!

Week #37

Purpose Pain

Suffering and difficulty seem to be necessary factors in anyone's quest for their purpose. Pain adds a dimension of maturity and reality that makes us stronger and more sensitive to the needs around us. It was written of Jesus: "He learned obedience from what he suffered" (Hebrews 5:8). If that's how Jesus learned obedience, you can be sure that we will learn the same way.

The Bible is full of stories of purposeful people who suffered and waited. Moses spent 40 years in the wilderness before he returned to Egypt to rescue his people. After Samuel had anointed him to be the new king, David spent 25 years waiting to replace the existing one. Joseph's story in the Old Testament is special to me. (Take the time to read his story for yourself in Genesis 37-50.)

I won't go into the entire story, but Joseph suffered for 22 years at the hands of family and associates in order to fulfill his purpose. Then he had to fulfill it in a foreign land under difficult circumstances. Things were so difficult that he named his second son "Ephraim," which means "God has made me fruitful in the land of my suffering."

Sometimes the suffering is in not being able to immediately fulfill your purpose once you find it. Another key source of suffering is the opposition that often comes from people close to you. Finally, you may suffer through some failure, having started out confident of success. Whatever the source of your pain, it is part of everyone's quest for their purpose. The pain will help you grow and deal with any pride; it will also connect you to the pain of others.

Are you in a difficult place? Then you're probably right where you need to be! You may want to study some historical person of purpose. What role did suffering have in their life? What role is it playing in your own life? God can still make you fruitful in the midst of your own land of suffering. I pray that your pain will lead to purpose and productivity, and that it won't last one day longer than it needs to last.

WEEK #38
Never Too Young

I've found that this generation of youth "connects" with the purpose message in a meaningful way. In Zimbabwe, one young lady came to the *Seven Steps* seminar and went home to begin writing a children's devotional. Other parents reported how their children went home and laid out plans to find their purpose, to the surprise and delight of their parents. I use my own daughter as another example. Since she was four, Deborah could sell anything. She usually outsold her classmates when her school had fundraising projects, and as a teenager, she got a job with Sears and Roebuck as a telemarketer. She won a district award from Sears for her work, even though she was only fifteen.

When she entered college, her mother and I were surprised that Deborah chose education as her major. After being in school for only a few weeks, she called home and told me that she had a "vision." As she was entering the people mover at her university, she "saw" herself getting on a plane. Deborah said she knew she was getting on that plane to go sell something to someone. She got off the people mover and transferred into the business school. When Deborah graduated, she went to work for a pharmaceutical company as a sales rep. They gave her a company car and generous benefits. My daughter is a young woman of purpose, and she doesn't have to suffer in the wrong job to find her way to fulfillment.

Recently I talked to a group of youth in England about purpose. I showed them, from the Bible, how many children and young people knew their purpose early in life. Joseph knew at 17 years of age that he would be the leader of his father's household. Samuel heard God's call when he was a child serving with Eli. David was a teenager when Samuel anointed him king of Israel. Daniel was a youth when he entered the service of the king of Babylon. And Mary, mother of Jesus, had an angel visit her while she was a teenager and change her life forever.

What does this have to do with you? If you have children or work with young people, talk to them about purpose and see how they respond. See if they don't readily connect with what you're saying. If you aren't numbered among the youth anymore, there's still hope. Jesus urged us all to be like children as we seek to enter His kingdom. Try to reconnect with your youthful ability to dream, to think about what you want to do in the future. Don't talk yourself out of it, but act like a child and live in that dream today. Then when you "wake up" from your dream, see what steps you can take to make that dream a reality.

Purpose is a hot topic in church and business circles. Many authors are writing, "You have a purpose…you have a purpose." When asked in return, "What is my purpose?" most respond, "You have a purpose." They can't really say anything more specific than that. My goal is to enlist an army of purposeful people who not only know their purpose but can also help others find their purpose. If you haven't already, I invite you to enlist in this purpose army, whether you're young or young at heart.

WEEK #39

God Wants More

It's interesting to study how Jesus used parables when He taught. Parables are stories with a moral or lesson, and there are 41 parables that are recorded in the first three gospels. I'm especially intrigued by the story found in Matthew 25:14-30. You may want to read the entire story, for I include only the last few verses here:

> Then the man who had received the one talent came. "Master," he said, "I knew that you are a hard man, harvesting where you have not sown and gathering where you have not scattered seed. So I was afraid and went out and hid your talent in the ground. See, here is what belongs to you." His master replied, "You wicked, lazy servant! So you knew that I harvest where I have not sown and gather where I have not scattered seed? Well then, you should have put my money on deposit with the bankers, so that when I returned I would have received it back with interest. Take the talent from him and give it to the one who has the ten talents. For everyone who has will be given more, and he will have an abundance. Whoever does not have, even what he has will be taken from him. And throw that worthless servant outside, into the darkness, where there will be weeping and gnashing of teeth" (Matthew 25:24-30).

The talents referred to here were monetary units and not gifts or abilities, so the three men in the parable received decreasing amounts of money. The master expected each of them to bring unspecified increase to what they were given. The first two did just that; the third man did not.

When the day of accounting came, the third man who did not manage to obtain any increase told the master why. He said that he was angry and afraid. Perhaps he was upset because the other two men got more money to work with than he did. The servant saw the master as a tyrant, expecting increase for which the master himself didn't labor. The servant took and hid the money and gave it back undiminished, unharmed, but without any increase. Upon hearing how difficult he was to work with, the master became angry and ordered the one talent to be taken away from the servant and given to the servant who had earned the largest increase.

This is the story of many people with whom I work. They are afraid of failure and would rather do nothing than the wrong thing. They play it safe and hope to not lose rather than to win. Here is a quote from Simon Kistemaker's book entitled *The Parables:*

> The servant entrusted with the one talent kept the deposit safely in a hidden place. He feared to put it to use, for he knew that his master would demand the talent from him upon his return. Fear, therefore, completely overshadowed love, trust, and faith. Fear is the opposite of confidence.
>
> The Christian who puts faith to work will reap immense dividends. He is not concerned about himself and his own interests, for whatever he owns belongs to the Lord and whatever he does he does for the Lord. No follower of Jesus can ever say that he lacks the gifts to be of service simply because he is not a Paul, Luther, Calvin, or Knox. The parable teaches that every servant has received gifts, "each according to his ability." Jesus knows the capability of every Christian, and he expects an increase.
>
> As with many other parables, specific details cannot

and should not be stressed and applied. Rather, the central message of faithfulness is important. The parable of the talents teaches that every believer has been endowed with gifts differing according to ability, and that these gifts must be put to use in God's service. In the kingdom of God everyone is expected to employ fully the gifts he has received. In God's kingdom there simply is no room for drones—only for worker bees.[12]

Which of the servants are you? Are you working in faith to bring increase to your world through your purpose and dreams, or are you afraid and hesitant? I trust that you will work hard to bring the faithful increase that is your right and duty as a follower of Jesus. After all, increase is your duty and, what's more, God's expectation.

WEEK #40
Just and Only

Let's take a look at the man named Nehemiah in the next few studies. If you remember from an earlier study, Nehemiah was an Old Testament builder and leader. When we read about Nehemiah, we learn that he was the cupbearer for the king in a land far from his home. Nehemiah says,

> Hanani, one of my brothers, came from Judah with some other men, and I questioned them about the Jewish remnant that survived the exile, and also about Jerusalem. They said to me, "Those who survived the exile and are back in the province are in great trouble and disgrace. The wall of Jerusalem is broken down, and its gates have been burned with fire." When I heard these things, I sat down and wept. For some days I mourned and fasted and prayed before the God of heaven (Nehemiah 1:2-4).

I'm not sure if Nehemiah realized that this visitor from his homeland would hold the key to Nehemiah's purpose. You may be searching for your purpose, but it may not be clear because history hasn't made it clear. Nehemiah couldn't know his purpose until Jerusalem was in disrepair and the people were in desperate straits. One day, a man appeared who gave Nehemiah a bad report about the condition of Jerusalem. This report, probably heard by many others, impacted Nehemiah more deeply than anyone else. This is similar to Winston Churchill, who was a politician all his life, but who didn't find his purpose until Nazi Germany threatened the world. It was then Churchill realized he had been born to save the Western world from the Nazis.

Notice how Nehemiah went about seeking clarification of his purpose. He stopped what he was doing and sat down. He cried, almost always a sure sign that someone is considering or close to purpose-related activities. Then Nehemiah prayed and even went without food. The issue of purpose is so powerful that it can often make you forget about food. Even Jesus said, "I have food to eat that you know nothing about" (John 4:32).

Then later in the story, Nehemiah went in to see the king. The king noticed that Nehemiah looked glum and said:

> So the king asked me, "Why does your face look so sad when you are not ill? This can be nothing but sadness of heart." I was very much afraid, but I said to the king, "May the king live forever! Why should my face not look sad when the city where my fathers are buried lies in ruins, and its gates have been destroyed by fire?" The king said to me, "What is it you want?" Then I prayed to the God of heaven, and I answered the king, "If it pleases the king and if your servant has found favor in his sight, let him send me to the city in Judah where my fathers are buried so that I can rebuild it" (Nehemiah 2:2-5).

It's important that you be ready to describe your purpose in one short, concise statement. If a king asks you what it is that you want, you shouldn't respond, "Well, uh, I sort of would like to, you know, well, I was hoping that I could, like maybe go to the mission field." Many people are so uncomfortable talking about themselves that they miss opportunities because they aren't clear or they're afraid to be specific. Not so with Nehemiah. He asked God for help and then he stated his purpose clearly: "Send me to the city in Judah where my fathers are buried so that I can rebuild it."

When I sit and help someone clarify their purpose, I try to listen carefully. Two words seem to occur regularly when people talk to me about purpose. They tell me that they "just" do this or "only" do that. "Just" and "only" are often gateways to a clear purpose statement, for we often look past the obvious in search of a more glamorous or dramatic purpose.

Nehemiah prayed for clarity and then he told the king, his supervisor, what he wanted to do. The king was inclined to help him. Make every effort to be clear and direct in your description of who you are and what you were created to do. If someone who has the power to help you fulfill your purpose asks, be ready to tell them what you need without apology. See the words "just" and "only" as keys to your life purpose and then you'll see that what you "only" do has the power to change your life and world.

WEEK #41
Handling Criticism

I've written about purpose and opposition before, but I learned some things from Nehemiah's life that may help you in your own search for purpose. As we saw in the previous study, Nehemiah was deeply moved by the poor conditions of his home city. After he fasted and prayed, he was able to clearly declare what he wanted to do while talking to his supervisor, the king. The king gave Nehemiah a leave of absence to go to Jerusalem, rebuild the walls, and resettle the inhabitants.

This is where his opposition appeared. There were people who had a vested interest in Jerusalem not being rebuilt, and they began to make life difficult for Nehemiah and his workers. I find it fascinating that often there's no opposition in your life until you start to fulfill your purpose as we saw earlier in the life of Joseph. Family, friends, church members, and coworkers—the people who know you best—then may tell you that you're crazy or misguided. They may even become actively involved in opposing the steps you are taking to fulfill your purpose.

Nehemiah's enemies used three tactics to keep him from his purpose: intimidation, confrontation, and criticism. Let's take a look at the criticism that came his way:

1. *They said he was rebellious.* "But when Sanballat the Horonite, Tobiah the Ammonite official, and Geshem the Arab heard about it, they mocked and ridiculed us. 'What is this you are doing?' they asked. 'Are you rebelling against the king?'" (Nehemiah 2:19). Often your efforts to fulfill your purpose are seen as going against someone else's plans for you. They will then accuse you of trying to do your "own thing" and portray you as an independent or a loner.

2. They said the job was too big for Nehemiah. "When Sanballat heard that we were rebuilding the wall, he became angry and was greatly incensed. He ridiculed the Jews, and in the presence of his associates and the army of Samaria, he said, 'What are those feeble Jews doing? Will they restore their wall? Will they offer sacrifices? Will they finish in a day? Can they bring the stones back to life from those heaps of rubble—burned as they are?'" (Nehemiah 4:1-2). Sometimes people get angry for no reason as you travel the road of your purpose. They try to tell you what you want to do is impossible and no one has ever done it before.

3. They said he was not capable. "Tobiah the Ammonite, who was at his side, said, 'What they are building—if even a fox climbed up on it, he would break down their wall of stones!'" (Nehemiah 4:3). Some people will tell you you're not that good or talented, that you don't have what it takes to make it in music, theater, business, ministry, missions, or any other field of endeavor that you desire to pursue.

Nehemiah learned to deal with his critics, and you'll need to learn to do that too if you're to succeed in fulfilling your purpose. Paul wrote something that encourages me:

> Am I now trying to win the approval of men, or of God? Or am I trying to please men? If I were still trying to please men, I would not be a servant of Christ (Galatians 1:10).

Your purpose is the will of God for your life. You don't need anyone's permission to do God's will; but in doing His will, you will encounter opposition and criticism. You must learn to deal with it and move on, for anyone who has done great things has had to do the same.

I trust that you will work for the praise of God and not let your opposition hinder you, not even the opposition from within. There are times when there's an internal critic that accuses you of the same three things that are outlined above. I urge you to move beyond external and internal criticism to take purposeful action in your life. Listen to your critics but don't take them too seriously. What God thinks is the only thing that matters at the end of the day.

WEEK #42

He Changed the "S" to "P"

I read a great book, entitled *Paul: The Traveler and Roman Citizen*, by William Ramsey. I love to read anything about the Apostle Paul because he was such a man of purpose. Paul was difficult to work with and had little patience for underachievers. Next to Jesus, however, no one played a greater role in the development of the early church than Paul. He was able to do so, not because he was smart (he was) or aggressive (he was), but because he was a man of purpose. When he went to the Gentiles, God went with him and the results were spectacular.

I was reading about Paul's first missionary journey to Cyprus and the Galatian region in Acts 13. When Paul confronted a magician who was trying to hinder his work, Luke (the writer of Acts) stated, "Then Saul, who was also called Paul . . ." (Acts 13:9). What a simple but powerful statement! It was 14 years since Saul had his dramatic encounter with Jesus on the Damascus road and now he stepped forward on the mission field and said, "My name is no longer Saul but Paul." It took Paul 14 years to realize who he was and what he was created to do, and when he did, he accepted his name change to Paul.

Think about it. Saul was a Roman citizen from the cross-cultural city of Tarsus. He knew four languages. Saul understood the Roman/Greek world of his day, and he was in some ways more comfortable in the Gentile world than he was in Jerusalem. Saul had legal rights as a Roman citizen—rights that Jesus did not have when He was crucified. Saul was a Jew *and* a Roman! In Cyprus, Saul stepped forward into his purpose e and from that point, he was known, and is still known today, as Paul. What a difference a one letter change from "S" to "P" made in world history!

That's the power of purpose. Nothing changed in Saul's life except how he saw himself in his mind. That was enough to have him boldly step forward and in essence say, "This is who I am. This is what I was created to do and be." From that point, his travels, letters and legacy have impacted the world for 2,000 years.

Who are you? What is your "name"? Are you ready to step forward and acknowledge who you are and what your past has shaped and prepared you to be today? Are you prepared to stop identifying with how others see you and make a statement of purpose for yourself? Now is the time to step out of the shadows of who you have been into the light of who God wants you to be. The world is waiting for the real you to emerge, and you may not have to do a lot to make that happen. After all, Paul simply accepted one letter change in his name and the rest is history. What little thing can you do that will enable you to embrace who you are? What are you waiting for?

WEEK #43

Stop Trying to Figure It Out

When I talk with people to help clarify their purpose, some are so stuck on one idea in their head they cannot follow what is in their heart. Consequently, their head is helping them see options but isn't helping them choose among them. If this describes where you are, this study is for you!

First and foremost, faith is what you use to find your purpose. When you start looking for your purpose, you must believe that you have one. That requires faith in the God of your purpose and not faith in your ability to figure out what it is. You must have faith that God is able to show you what your purpose is. This sounds so basic, but it's a critical step. I talk to many people who are praying to know their purpose, but they don't really believe that God is showing them what it is. They dismiss the "spiritual" evidence of joy, passion, and talent in the light of their rational understanding of the evidence. If you're praying to know your purpose, why are you so skeptical that God is answering? If you're seeking the mind of Christ, why are you surprised that you may have it? I'm reminded of a simple concept that Jesus taught:

> "Which of you fathers, if your son asks for a fish, will give him a snake instead? Or if he asks for an egg, will give him a scorpion? If you then, though you are evil, know how to give good gifts to your children, how much more will your Father in heaven give the Holy Spirit to those who ask him!" (Luke 11:11-13).

I've known people who ask what their purpose is and then are released from their jobs the next week. That's difficult, but I urge them to see that as an answer to prayer. I've talked to others who prayed and then had a perfect stranger come up to them to give them an important clue in understanding their purpose. Do you expect this to happen to you? If you ask your Father for purpose, do you expect the unexpected? When it comes, will you receive it?

Faith is the means not only to find but also to fulfill your purpose. I talk to people who haven't written a book because they don't know who will publish or purchase their book. Faith requires that you do what you can do and then trust God to do what only He can do. You write; God publishes. You create; God sells. If you stop taking the steps you *can* take because you don't understand how the latter steps can ever happen, you are guilty of trying to figure out how everything will work out. In short, you don't have faith and you're allowing your lack of faith to hinder what you can do today. I can only remind you of one of my favorite verses: "In the same way, faith by itself, if it is not accompanied by action, is dead" (James 2:17).

If you don't take the steps only *you* can take, don't expect God to take the steps only *He* can take. In many ways, how God responds to you is determined by how you respond to God. I hope this will help you to stop trying to figure out what to do and to just do it. I hope this will also help you see what is happening in your life as an answer to prayer, an answer that you aren't supposed to analyze but act upon.

Week #44

Moses: "Here I Am!"

One day, while reading Exodus 3, I noticed that Moses said seven things during his encounter with the Lord at the burning bush. The first thing Moses said to the Lord involved three simple words: "Here I am." Those words may not seem very important, but they are. Let's examine these words more closely and see how they can help you as you walk out your purpose.

I did a quick study of others who said "Here I am" and found out that Abraham said it twice when God spoke to him to sacrifice Isaac (see Genesis 22:1, 7, 11). Then Jacob said it in Genesis 46:2 when God spoke to him to go down to Egypt. Finally, Samuel said it when the Lord called him to a prophetic purpose (see 1 Samuel 3:4). What's so important about these words? I think they're critical to anyone who is on search for their purpose, expecting to hear or see something from God.

"Here I am" signifies that you're ready to do what God wants before you know what it is. It says that you're ready and trust whatever God shows you to do. When you're looking for your purpose, you can't have a "Huh?" attitude. You must have a "Here I am" attitude if you hope to clarify your purpose.

I once knew someone struggling to find their purpose, and a pastor gave them good advice. He said, "During your search, can you thank God for your purpose before you know what it is? Can you believe that God will show it to you and say thank you in advance?" I think that advice was "Here I am" advice. You present yourself at attention, just like a good soldier awaiting orders. And then you wait to hear what they are.

As you pursue your purpose, you need to couple a "Here I am" attitude with a "Here I am" faith. Read the passages that are referenced above and study the search of Moses, Jacob and Samuel. Then prepare yourself for the God of your purpose to reveal it. When and how He does that, I can't say. But "Here I am" faith will help make it happen.

WEEK #45

Moses: "Who Am I?"

In the previous study, we looked at the first of seven comments that Moses made when he had his encounter with the Lord at the burning bush. We saw that his first comment was, "Here I am," and saw that we need to have a ready attitude to listen and do whatever God wants us to do.

Now let's look at his second comment: "But Moses said to God, 'Who am I, that I should go to Pharaoh and bring the Israelites out of Egypt?'" (Exodus 3:11).

It seems that Moses had something in common with many people, and that was low self-esteem. God had just confirmed to him his purpose, a purpose that he already knew; yet Moses immediately began to tell God why he wasn't the one to go to Egypt. There was a man standing before a burning bush, hearing the voice of God, and he was telling God that he was insignificant. Does this sound familiar? Don't you and I often do the same thing?

We pray to do God's will and fulfill our purpose and then we're surprised when God agrees. When we sense our purpose, we have a tendency to present reasons why we can't do it. We might say, "Who am I, Lord, for I don't have the money, education, experience, permission, or talent to do Your will?"

Are you struggling with low self-esteem or lack of confidence? Then, first of all, you can take consolation that Moses struggled with the same things and still went on to do great things for God. That alone should encourage you to move on and fulfill your purpose. But if you need some additional encouragement, consider these verses:

1. *"As God's fellow workers we urge you not to receive God's*

grace in vain" (2 Corinthians 6:1-2). You are not alone. When you work for God, you work with God. He is your co-worker! If it's only you, you may have cause for concern. God is working with you in whatever it is He asks you to do.

2. *"I have been crucified with Christ and I no longer live, but Christ lives in me. The life I live in the body, I live by faith in the Son of God, who loved me and gave himself for me"* (Galatians 2:20-21). More than simply being *with you*, God lives *in you*. You can learn how to surrender to Jesus who lives in you and works through you. That makes you a carrier of Someone special who empowers you to fulfill your purpose.

3. *"But we have the mind of Christ"* (1 Corinthians 2:16). If one of the effects of Christ living in you is to have His mind, why are you so surprised and doubtful that you may have it? When you realize that you have this mind, you will have more confidence in your ability, or rather God's ability to fulfill the task that's before you.

Now is a good time to face your lack of confidence and low self-esteem. Honestly assess where you are in regard to God's purpose for your life. If you are thinking or saying, "Who am I?" then it's time to answer that question, relying on truths found in the three verses shown. Move beyond your limitations into the vast possibilities of those people who have stopped putting faith in their own abilities to put their faith in God.

WEEK #46

Moses: "Who Sent Me?"

Now let's look at Moses' third comment:

> "Suppose I go to the Israelites and say to them, 'The God of your fathers has sent me to you,' and they ask me, 'What is his name?' Then what shall I tell them?" (Exodus 3:13).

I think Moses was stalling for time when he asked this question. He was basically saying, "I'm not ready to go. I don't have all the necessary information. I need to know more about God. I need to be better equipped." I've encountered people doing the same thing when they find their purpose or have an idea. They often tell me, "I'm praying about it," but when I probe, I find out they aren't really. Or they tell me, "I don't have the education," or "I don't pray enough," or "I need to get this fixed or right in my life before I go and do." These are excuses that delay doing what it is that is before us.

I'm not saying that you don't need more training, that you don't need to pray more, or that you don't need to know more about the Lord. None of these issues disqualify you from doing God's will today. Nor do they represent something that can't be addressed *while* you are fulfilling your purpose instead of *before* you fulfill it. Many people are trying to figure out *how* to do God's will before they actually begin. Seldom is that possible.

Hebrews 11:34-35 states, "Whose weakness was turned to strength; and who became powerful in battle and routed foreign armies." I thought it interesting that the heroes of faith didn't wait until they had strength; rather they received strength *when* they entered the battle. Too many people say,

"If God gives me strength, I'll go and do it," but God says, "If you go and do it, I'll give you the strength (or wisdom, power or ability) that you need." If you're waiting until you're ready to go, you may never be ready to go. At least part of the preparation is proceeding to work on what you're trying to get ready to do.

Are you procrastinating and delaying action on what God wants you to do? What excuse have you come up with that sounds logical? Are you ready to face the truth of why you are delaying? I hope that you are, for God knew your weakness when He first spoke to you. In spite of that, He is holding out a chance for you to fulfill your purpose. Are you ready to stop delaying and begin acting? Today could be the day when you finally stop asking questions, trying to figure it all out. For your sake, I hope it is.

Week #47

Moses: "What If I Fail?"

Let's continue our studies on Moses and his comments during his encounter with the Lord at the burning bush. Now it's time to look at his fourth comment: "What if they do not believe me or listen to me and say, 'The Lord did not appear to you'?" (Exodus 4:1) Moses was asking, "What if I fail? What if I'm obedient, but the people are not?" From my own life and experience as a purpose coach, I'm ready to declare that fear of failure is the primary stumbling block for people trying to be more purposeful and productive. You can be so afraid to do the wrong thing that you do nothing, missing opportunities that could be significant.

Are you afraid of failure? Is that what stands between you and your attempt to fulfill your purpose or achieve your goal? Let's look at a famous quote from American president, Teddy Roosevelt, which addressed the issue of failure:

> It is not the critic who counts; not the man who points out how the strong man stumbles, or where the doer of deeds could have done them better. The credit belongs to the man who is actually in the arena, whose face is marred by dust and sweat and blood; who strives valiantly; who errs, and comes up short again and again, because there is no effort without error and shortcoming; but who does actually strive to do the deeds; who knows the great enthusiasms, the great devotions; who spends himself in a worthy cause; who at the best knows in the end the triumph of high achievement, and who at the worse, if he fails, at least fails while daring

greatly, so that his place shall never be with those cold and timid souls who know neither victory nor defeat.

I'm of the opinion that it's better to fail trying to do something than succeed at doing nothing, for the latter isn't really success at all. I've been too concerned in the past with what other people thought. I've also been too concerned with trying *not* to fail instead of trying to succeed.

Are you ready to face your fear of failure? There's only one way to do that, and that's to do something about what you've always said you would do one day. I'm writing to tell you that the "one day" is here and now. I've quoted James 2:17 many times to many people: "In the same way, faith by itself, if it is not accompanied by action, is dead." Take some immediate action that will help you overcome your fear of failure and do something that could change your world.

WEEK #48

Moses: "Just a Staff"

We continue our study of Moses' comments during his encounter with the burning bush. It's time to look at his fifth comment, which was an answer to a question God asked Moses: "'What is that in your hand?' 'A staff,' he [Moses] replied" (Exodus 4:2). Moses was concerned he would fail because of all the things he didn't have. In his mind, Moses didn't have enough knowledge about God, he lacked the confidence, he was too old, and he wouldn't be able to respond to the peoples' questions. God asked him a simple question: "What do you have?"

When God assigned your purpose, He knew your gifts, strengths, and weaknesses. If God was content with that package, why should they be of concern to you? People regularly tell me reasons why they can't fulfill their purpose or dreams. They tell me that they lack the education, they're too young or too old, they don't have the money, or they aren't gifted enough. Have you ever said any of those things? God isn't asking you for an inventory of things that you don't have; He's more concerned that you allow Him to use you and what you *do* have.

Moses went to Egypt with that staff in obedience to God's command. He fulfilled his purpose with what he had in his hand. You will fulfill your purpose the same way. Moses was honest with God; he told Him what he had. God went on to show him that it was enough. (Read Exodus 4:3-9 on your own.) Will you allow God to prove to you that you do have what it takes to do His will as long as you submit what you have to Him?

You need to move beyond the realm of excuses to the kingdom of obedience, face your fears, and obey God. In the process, you need to surrender what you do have to God's empowering touch so that you will be equipped to fulfill your purpose. Moses only had a staff in his hand and it was enough. What do you have in your hand that will enable you to do what you were created to do?

WEEK #49

Moses: Excuses, Excuses

We've almost completed our study of Moses' comments during his encounter with the burning bush. His sixth comment was: "Moses said to the Lord, 'O Lord, I have never been eloquent, neither in the past nor since you have spoken to your servant. I am slow of speech and tongue'" (Exodus 4:10).

With this sixth comment, Moses moved from honest questioning to procrastination. He was working hard to come up with some excuse, any excuse so that he wouldn't have to go to Egypt. If you look hard enough, you'll always find a reason that could exempt you from fulfilling your purpose. We saw some of them in the previous study. Some more reasons I hear on a regular basis are: "I don't like to speak in front of people; my spouse/pastor/leader/supervisor doesn't feel good about me doing that; I'm not sure it's God's will; I'm waiting on the Lord's timing." I've heard these reasons many times, and God has heard them even more often.

I especially want to address the last excuse: "I'm waiting on the Lord's timing." I heard a leader say one time, "The need that you see is your call." He meant that seeing a need that exists is often the only "call" you are going to receive. When I teach about purpose, I ask what is it that you see that you assume everyone else sees. In most cases, everyone does not see what you see. Seeing it then requires that you do something about it, without over-spiritualizing the process. God, who has given you the ability to see the need, will also equip you to address that need. The Lord responded to Moses:

> The Lord said to him, "Who gave man his mouth? Who makes him deaf or mute? Who gives him

sight or makes him blind? Is it not I, the Lord? Now go; I will help you speak and will teach you what to say" (Exodus 4:11-12).

Perhaps God is saying the same thing to you. He may be directing you to "go" and "do." As you go, He will help you speak or do whatever it is that He wants you to do. Stop procrastinating and finding excuses to justify your delay. The good news is that it isn't too late. The God of your purpose is extending another opportunity to do His will. Don't disappoint Him or make Him find someone else. You can do it. What's more, you must do it if you are to be a person of purpose.

WEEK #50
Moses: Into the Game

Let's begin with a story from the world of sports. Several years ago, a professional basketball game was in the final seconds. The coach called time out and issued a play that he hoped would win the game. When play resumed, however, only four of his players were in the game. The fifth player, who was also the star, refused to go back in because he wasn't slated to take the winning shot. He forced the coach to put someone else in although his team won anyway. Needless to say, players, writers and fans criticized that player for his selfish behavior.

As we look at Moses' seventh comment, we see that Moses, having exhausted all the excuses and questions he could think of, simply refused to go to Egypt. "But Moses said, 'O Lord, please send someone else to do it'" (Exodus 4:13). In essence, Moses said "no" to God! Moses refused to go into the game just like that basketball player. And what was God's response? "Then the Lord's anger burned against Moses" (Exodus 4:14). I hope I never make God angry, but this story proves that it can happen. God is patient but there are limitations to His patience, and we're never quite sure when we will reach them.

People ask me all the time, "Can you refuse your purpose?" and my answer is always, "Yes!" Consider these two passages as examples: "But the Pharisees and experts in the law rejected God's purpose for themselves" (Luke 7:30); and "As God's fellow workers we urge you not to receive God's grace in vain" (2 Corinthians 6:1-2).

You can receive the grace of God's purpose in vain, choosing to ignore or do nothing with it. You can sit on your gifts, choosing to remain in the comfort zone of life rather than experiencing the discomfort of new faith experiences. You can be so afraid of doing the wrong thing that you choose to do nothing instead.

God had answered and addressed each of Moses' questions and concerns so that the real reason for Moses' reluctance could be revealed: Moses just didn't want to do it. Like that star basketball player, Moses just didn't want to go into the game.

How about you? Are you testing God's patience through delay and excuses? The good news is that after Moses said this, God assigned Aaron to go with Moses and then sent them both on their way to Egypt. If you confess that you don't want to fulfill your purpose, and that you're scared, lazy, or lack confidence, then the Lord will still help you! You're not alone in your search for purpose; God is with you, even in your hesitancy. All you have to do is acknowledge where you are and ask God's help. He will do the rest. It's time to face reality and move on to do great things for God, just as Moses did. God wants you in the game. Will you go?

Week #51

Celebrate a Failure

I have an idea for an international holiday that we could call "Celebrate a Failure Day." Surprised? Since failure is a common experience among all people, then it must serve some purpose in our lives. I think it comes to teach and train us, to prepare us for the ultimate success that will come if we don't give up. Here are ideas I have for this new holiday:

- If you are a pastor, talk about failure and its role in the life of the believer. Make sure you are clear that it is spiritual to fail.
- Spend time talking with your family, and especially your children, about failure. You may want to focus on one particular failure in your own life and what you learned from it. This will free your children from the false sense that failure is to be avoided at all costs. Maybe you can have a family failure party! Make sure you laugh a lot, even at yourself.
- If you are in a small group setting, spend some time talking about your failures, how you view failure, and whether you are afraid of failure now.
- In your business, talk about your recent failures and what you have learned from them. See if these failures have caused coworkers to avoid failure, thus limiting the ability of your business to experiment and grow.

Why am I proposing this unusual action? One business leader said, "Make as many mistakes as you can as quickly as possible. In that way, you'll learn and stay ahead of your competition." When Thomas Watson, founder of IBM, was informed that one of his subordinates had just made a million-dollar mistake, he was asked whether he would terminate that employee. Watson replied, "Heavens no! I just invested $1 million in his education."

As I study the books of Acts, I've noticed that Paul preached one of his greatest sermons in Athens (see Acts 17:15-34), yet he saw very few results. Many feel he went on from there to Corinth a discouraged man. It was in Corinth he experienced tremendous results and even had a visitation from the Lord, who told him, "Do not be afraid any longer, but go on speaking and do not be silent" (Acts 18:9, NAS).

It occurred to me that the Lord often "appeared" to Paul when he was at his lowest and needed encouragement. It was because Paul attempted to do so much that he encountered so much failure and probable depression. It was at those points when God Himself undertook to encourage His man.

Perhaps you are discouraged, or depressed, over a failure. If so, you're ripe for a visitation from God; He's not far from the downhearted, and you qualify. Why not expect a miracle that will encourage your heart and help you overcome your fear or sense of failure? Maybe you can encourage someone else who is struggling with their own sense of humanity and failure.

We must move beyond our ability to tolerate failure to a place where we can celebrate it by talking about it and learning from it. So don't wait for the holiday to be officially proclaimed. Start celebrating failure today and move through failure to a more meaningful, successful life and career.

WEEK #52
Hit It Hard and Wish It Well

Years ago, when I lived in the southern United States, I played a lot of softball. Softball is a game similar to American baseball, but the ball is bigger and the pitcher throws it more slowly and underhand. I wasn't a good player, nor was my team very successful. There was one team that was very good, and they defeated our teams most of the time, year after year. They didn't look as sharp as we did because we got new uniforms almost every year. We practiced weekly, yet we never saw them on the practice field. They just knew how to win.

One night we met with some of their players to interview them and see if we could gain the secret of their success. We asked many questions, but then our coach asked their best hitter, "When you're at bat, do you have an offensive philosophy? Do you try to hit it over the fence or do you try to advance the runners one base at a time?" The man gave our coach a surprised look and announced, "We don't have any philosophy. We just hit it hard and wish it well."

As you seek to fulfill your purpose and be productive, this may be a good strategy to follow. You may just need to "hit it hard and wish it well." In softball, sometimes you can do everything just right and not get to first base. Other times you can do things wrong, but the ball falls in the right spot and you can win the game. Maybe you're waiting for perfection before you try something, or you're frustrated that you've done everything correctly, but things haven't work out. This week you need to overcome your hesitancy or discouragement and go to bat one more time.

This "hit it hard and wish it well" is a principle found in

the Bible. The writer of Ecclesiastes wrote about it thousands of years ago:

> If clouds are full of water, they pour rain upon the earth. Whether a tree falls to the south or to the north, in the place where it falls, there will it lie. Whoever watches the wind will not plant; whoever looks at the clouds will not reap. As you do not know the path of the wind, or how the body is formed in a mother's womb, so you cannot understand the work of God, the Maker of all things. Sow your seed in the morning, and at evening let not your hands be idle, for you do not know which will succeed, whether this or that, or whether both will do equally well (Ecclesiastes 11:3-6).

Recently I spent some time improving *The Seven Steps of a PurposeQuest* seminar that I teach. My point is that I did something and now I'm going back to make it better. I conduct a seminar and "hit it hard and wish it well." Now I want you to take some dream, project, or idea, and do the same. You may strike out, but you may also hit a home run. I hope that the coming days bring you closer to the fulfillment of what is in your heart to do or be. Hit it hard and wish it well!

End Notes

[1] Robert K. Greenleaf, *Seeker and Servant: Reflections on Religious Leadership* (San Francisco: Jossey-Bass Publishers, 1996), p 104.

[2] Richard Leider and David A. Shapiro, *Whistle While You Work* (San Francisco: Berrett-Koehler Publishers, 2001), page 35.

[3] *Ibid.*, page 35.

[4] Laurence Boldt, *How to Find the Work You Love* (New York: Penguin Books, 1996), page 1.

[5] *Ibid.*, page 20.

[6] Henri Nouwen, *Making All Things New* (San Francisco: Harper SanFrancisco, 1981), page 67.

[7] Brian Mahan, *Forgetting Ourselves on Purpose* (San Francisco: Jossey-Bass, 2002), page 33.

[8] Julia Cameron, *The Artist's Way: A Spiritual Path to Higher Creativity* (New York: J. P. Tarcher, 2002), page 17.

[9] Abraham Maslow, *The Farther Reaches of Human Nature* (New York: Peter Smith Publishers, 1983), page 34.

[10] Os Guinness, *Entrepreneurs of Life: Faith and the Venture of Purposeful Living* (Colorado Springs: Navpress, 2001), page 190.

[11] *Christian History Magazine*, Issue 2: John Wesley, page 34.

[12] Simon Kistemaker, *The Parables: Understanding the Stories That Jesus Told* (Grand Rapids: Baker Books, 1980), pages 124-125.

About John W. Stanko

John founded a personal and leadership development company, called *PurposeQuest*, in 2001 and today travels the world to speak, consult and inspire leaders and people everywhere. From 2001-2008, he spent six months a year in Africa and still enjoys visiting and working on that continent. Most recently, John founded Urban Press, a publishing service designed to tell stories of the city, from the city and to the city. John is the author of 75 books.

Keep In Touch With John W. Stanko

www.purposequest.com
www.johnstanko.us
www.stankobiblestudy.com
www.stankomondaymemo.com

or via email at johnstanko@gmail.com

John also does extensive relief and community development work in Kenya. You can see some of his projects at www.purposequest.com/donate

PurposeQuest International
PO Box 8882
Pittsburgh, PA 15221-0882

Additional Titles In The *Unlocking* Series By John W. Stanko

Unlocking the Power of Your Creativity
Unlocking the Power of Your Productivity
Unlocking the Power of You
Unlocking the Power of Your Thinking
Unlocking the Power of Your Faith

More Books by John Stanko

A Daily Dose of Proverbs

A Daily Taste of Proverbs

Changing the Way We Do Church

I Wrote This Book on Purpose

Life Is A Gold Mine: Can You Dig It?

Strictly Business

The Faith Files, Volume 1

The Faith Files, Volume 2

The Faith Files, Volume 3

The Leadership Walk

The Price of Leadership

What Would Jesus Ask You Today?

Your Life Matters

Live the Word Commentary: Matthew

Live the Word Commentary: Mark

Live the Word Commentary: Luke

Live the Word Commentary: John

Live the Word Commentary: Acts

Live the Word Commentary: Romans

Live the Word Commentary: 1 & 2 Corinthians

Live the Word Commentary: Galatians, Ephesians, Philippians, Colossians, Philemon

Live the Word Commentary: 1 & 2 Thessalonians, 1 & 2 Timothy, and Titus

Live the Word Commentary: Hebrews

Live the Word Commentary: Revelation

Ediciones en Español

Cambiando la Manera de Hacer Iglesia

La Vida Es Una Mina De Oro: Te Atreves A Cavarla?

No Leas Estes Libro: (A Menos Que Quieras Convertirte E Un Mejor Líder)

Fuero lo Viejo, Adentro lo Nuevo

Gemas de Propósito

Ven a Adorarlo: Preparándonos para Emmanuel

Printed in the USA
CPSIA information can be obtained
at www.ICGtesting.com
CBHW070147220124
3592CB00005B/23